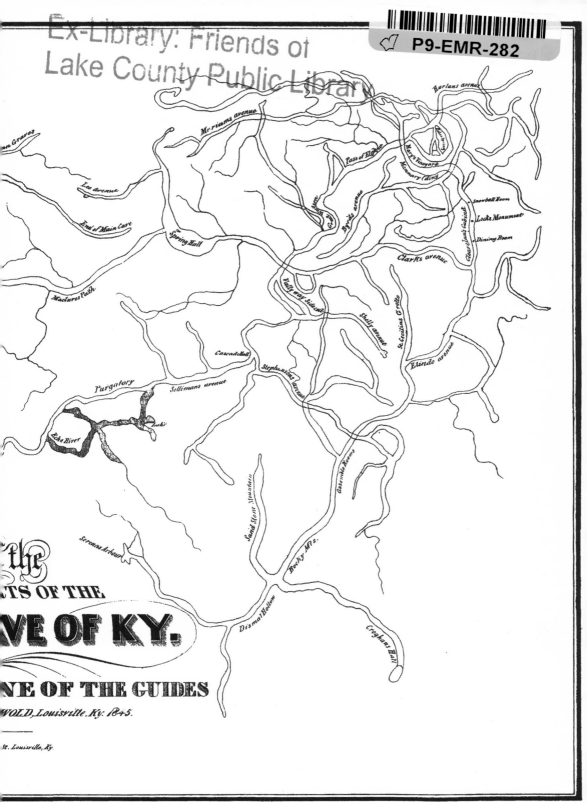

the

TS OF THE

VE OF KY.

NE OF THE GUIDES

WOLD, Louisville, Ky: 1845.

St. Louisville, Ky.

the Clerks office for the district of Kentucky

Journey to the Bottomless Pit

JOURNEY
to the
BOTTOMLESS PIT

The Story of Stephen Bishop *&* Mammoth Cave

ELIZABETH MITCHELL

illustrations by
KELLYN ALDER

VIKING

VIKING
Published by Penguin Group
Penguin Young Readers Group, 345 Hudson Street, New York, New York 10014, U.S.A.
Penguin Group (Canada), 10 Alcorn Avenue, Toronto, Ontario, Canada M4V 3B2
(a division of Pearson Penguin Canada Inc.)
Penguin Books Ltd, 80 Strand, London WC2R 0RL, England
Penguin Ireland, 25 St Stephen's Green, Dublin 2, Ireland (a division of Penguin Books Ltd)
Penguin Group (Australia), 250 Camberwell Road, Camberwell, Victoria 3124, Australia
(a division of Pearson Australia Group Pty Ltd)
Penguin Books India Pvt Ltd, 11 Community Centre, Panchsheel Park, New Delhi - 110 017, India
Penguin Group (NZ), Cnr Airborne and Rosedale Roads, Albany, Auckland, New Zealand
(a division of Pearson New Zealand Ltd)
Penguin Books (South Africa) (Pty) Ltd, 24 Sturdee Avenue, Rosebank, Johannesburg 2196, South Africa

Penguin Books Ltd, Registered Offices: 80 Strand, London WC2R 0RL, England

Published in 2004 by Viking, a division of Penguin Young Readers Group

3 5 7 9 10 8 6 4 2

Text copyright © Betsy Mitchell, 2004
Illustrations copyright © Kelynn Alder, 2004
All rights reserved

LIBRARY OF CONGRESS CATALOGING-IN-PUBLICATION DATA
Mitchell, Betsy, date–
Journey to the bottomless pit : the story of Stephen Bishop and Mammoth Cave / by Betsy Mitchell ;
illustrations by Kelynn Alder.
p. cm.
Summary: In 1838, as the nation struggles with issues of slavery, seventeen-year-old
Stephen Bishop serves his master as a guide in Kentucky's Mammoth Cave and
spends his free time exploring and discovering new passages and rooms.
ISBN 0-670-05908-0 (hardcover)
1. Mammoth Cave (Ky.)—Juvenile fiction. [1. Mammoth Cave (Ky.)—Fiction. 2. Caves—Fiction.
3. Slavery—Fiction. 4. Kentucky—History—1865—-Fiction.] I. Alder, Kelynn, ill. II. Title.
PZ7.M6883Jo 2004
[Fic]—dc22
2004001651

Printed in U.S.A.

Set in Bulmer
Designed by Kelley McIntyre

Artwork appearing on end papers, title page, and page viii
courtesy of the National Park Service.

Title page: Stephen Bishop leads a tour through Mammoth Cave.

To my grandfather,
John L. Mitchell,
who first took me to Mammoth Cave

CONTENTS

An engraving of Stephen Bishop
from the nineteenth century

To the Reader

The events of Stephen Bishop's life are presented in this book with as much factual accuracy as the author could manage, given the historical documents available. Please note that the dialogue is not reproduced from any source. Newspaper articles written about Stephen Bishop's discoveries never quoted Stephen himself. Sometimes he was referred to by name; more often he was called simply "the guide."

However, the writers whom Stephen conducted on tours were obviously impressed by him. The author's sources of information for this book include several firsthand reports written in the 1840s and 1850s. Travel writers and other visitors to Mammoth Cave often mentioned Stephen's lively personality, his quiet self-confidence and sense of humor, and his knowledge of the cave.

The author would like to thank Mammoth Park ranger/guides Joy Medley Lyons and Charles DeCroix, historian Bob Ward, and Vickie Carson of the Mammoth Cave Public Information Office for their contributions to this manuscript and its accuracy. Any errors herein are the author's, not theirs. In addition, thank you to the National Speleological Society for access to its videotape collection.

Journey to the Bottomless Pit

The New Guide

THE YOUNG SLAVE brushed aside branches and vines as he followed his master down the trail. Today he would start learning to guide visitors through Mammoth Cave. He was excited, but he was worried as well. Would he do a good job?

Seventeen-year-old Stephen Bishop had seen many caves in his life. He had grown up in the state of Kentucky, and Kentucky is full of caves, from animal dens in the sides of hills to holes larger than a house. But Mammoth Cave was so big that people came from all over to see it. And now it belonged to Stephen's master, Franklin Gorin.

Mr. Gorin led the way. He talked to Stephen as they crossed a wooden bridge over a small stream.

"I want everything to be ready by the end of April," he said. "That means you, too. You have to learn the trails quickly so you can start leading tours."

1

Franklin Gorin was a lawyer, but he was not a rich man. He had agreed to buy Mammoth Cave for $5,000. He had paid the first $1,000, but he needed to earn the rest of the money by charging people to tour the underground cavern.

Young Stephen had lived with his mother and his brother on Gorin's property in Glasgow, Kentucky. But Gorin reasoned that he could make more money on every tour if he used Stephen as a guide. He didn't have to pay Stephen, the way he would have to pay a free man. That is why he brought Stephen to the cave.

It was the year 1838, and about 180,000 slaves lived in Kentucky. Most toiled in the fields, clearing land, planting and weeding crops, and taking care of livestock. House slaves worked long hours inside their masters' homes, cooking, cleaning, and caring for the children.

A few slaves were taught a useful trade such as blacksmithing, fancy sewing, or cobbling shoes. But no one that Stephen knew had ever worked as a cave guide. Stephen felt proud that Mr. Gorin thought he could do this job.

Mr. Gorin carried one lantern and Stephen carried another. Both lanterns were filled with lard oil. Stephen also carried a bag over his shoulder. Inside were a tin box filled with matches, some spare wicks for the lamp, a canister filled with more oil, and enough lunch for two men. Mr. Gorin had told Stephen he would spend all day in the cave.

They rounded a bend in the trail, pushing past branches that were just sprouting new leaves. Now Stephen could hear the sound of someone sawing wood. In a clearing ahead of them he saw a group of men at work under the shade of a big tree. They were splitting logs and shaping boards.

Stephen recognized two of the men. They were slaves who usually worked at Mr. Gorin's house in Glasgow, fixing fences and doing carpentry.

"How are things coming, Tapscott?" Mr. Gorin called to the man in charge.

"Just fine, sir," the carpenter answered. "We'll have this railing finished in another few days."

While Mr. Gorin talked to Mr. Tapscott, Stephen noticed something very strange. The day was warm, warm enough that he didn't need any kind of a coat. But all of a sudden he could feel a chilly breeze coming from somewhere nearby. He looked around, puzzled.

Mr. Gorin noticed him. "You feel it, don't you?" he asked Stephen. "That's air blowing out of the cave. It's always nice and cool down there. Even on the hottest summer day, you'll feel as though you're stepping into the middle of October. "

Stephen followed Mr. Gorin around one more curve in the trail. There, an amazing sight met his eyes.

Stephen was facing a steep hillside. The hill was made of layers of rock, but it looked as though many layers had fallen away, leaving a huge opening downhill from where he was standing. Bushes and trees grew all around the opening, and a small stream cascaded from the top. It was the mouth of Mammoth Cave.

"The first job is to build a stairway down into the entrance, so that people can get inside safely," Mr. Gorin said to Stephen. "We've already measured eight miles of cave passage. People will pay well for tours, once we let them know we're ready for business. Come now. Here's someone for you to meet."

A young white man who had been watching the workers came over to join Stephen and Mr. Gorin. Mr. Gorin shook the man's hand and handed him the lantern he had been carrying.

"This is Archibald Miller," Mr. Gorin told Stephen. "He's been a guide here for about five years, and his daddy was a guide, too. You mind him well, and he'll teach you what you need to know."

Gorin turned back to the trail. He was headed to the top of the hill, where another gang of laborers was repairing and enlarging an old inn. Mammoth was located nine miles from the main stagecoach line between Louisville, Kentucky, and Nashville, Tennessee, and Gorin hoped that many travelers would stop to see his cave.

Archibald Miller looked Stephen up and down. Other men had done this before, making Stephen feel like a plow mule or a milk cow they were thinking of buying. But Mr. Miller just seemed to be taking his measure.

Miller looked only a few years older than Stephen. *If you learned this cave, then I can, too,* Stephen said to himself. For a moment he thought of his mother and brother back in Glasgow. They were so proud he had been chosen as a guide. Up until now, only white men had led visitors into Mammoth Cave.

"You'll need a good pair of boots," Mr. Miller said at last. "The cave floor is rough and rocky in a lot of places. I'll tell Mr. Gorin."

Mr. Miller and Stephen stopped at the edge of the deep hole. Steps made of broken rock led downward. A new wooden handrail extended part of the way, but below that Stephen had to be careful. The stream that ran off the top of the hillside fell alongside the steps. It splashed into a natural pond at the bottom of the stairway.

"This is where the visitors will fill their canteens," said Mr. Miller. "There is hardly any water inside the cave. Here, fill these up." He handed over two water bottles and waited while Stephen filled them to the top. They slung the bottles over their shoulders and Miller led the way forward.

Stephen gazed up as they stepped into the huge mouth of the cave. He felt very strange. Part of him was excited to be going into this new and very different place. But another part of him was scared. He had not imagined the cave would be so big. It looked very dark inside. What if he lost his way in the passages? What if other people got lost following him?

No time for worrying now. A dirt path led past the waterfall and into the cave. The opening began to narrow.

The cold air was all around him now, rushing out of the cave mouth. "It's no good lighting the lanterns until you're inside," Miller told him. "The wind blows them right out. Always carry

A new wooden handrail extended part of the way,
but below that Stephen had to be careful.

a good supply of oil and wicks. And keep all the lanterns clean and dry. We don't want anyone telling horror stories about getting lost in the dark." Stephen agreed with that!

The breeze blew fiercely as they passed through a narrow opening. Then they stopped to light the lanterns. Stephen looked over his shoulder. The cave mouth was not far behind him, but already the daylight could hardly be seen.

He held up his lantern and looked around.

They were in a low tunnel made of rock. The pathway underfoot was smooth clay. Overhead, the roof formed a rocky arch. Archibald Miller's lantern bobbed ahead of him.

"This part of the cave is called the Narrows," Miller said. He turned around. Stephen had stopped to touch the rocky wall alongside the trail. It felt chilly and damp.

"Don't lag behind, Stephen. That's how people get lost in here," Miller told him. "You'll have plenty of time to look around later. Today I'm going to show you the Church."

Church? What kind of strange church could be inside a cave? Stephen followed quickly. His eyes were getting used to the lamplight now. He could see a low, rocky roof overhead and rock walls on both sides of the pathway.

The narrow passageway was beginning to widen. The cave floor sloped gently downhill. Stephen noticed some wooden pipes running along the floor, and a pair of wagon ruts leading deeper into the cave. He wondered what animal had pulled a wagon into this strange place.

7

Suddenly the Narrows ended and Stephen could see only a great dark space in front of him.

Archibald Miller bent over a pile of broken-up wood. "Give me a hand," he said. Together they stacked enough wood to build a small fire. When the flame caught in the wood, Miller stood up and threw his arm wide.

"This is the first big room in the cave. We call it the Rotunda. Do you know that word?"

"No, sir." Stephen liked the sound of it, though. He loved learning new words.

"It means a large room with a high, domed ceiling." Miller raised his lantern.

Stephen looked up, and his eyes widened. Now he could see a vast rocky roof. It curved smoothly across a space so wide Stephen could not see any other wall from where he stood. The little fire they had built could not possibly light up this enormous room.

"The Rotunda is two hundred feet long, and the ceiling is as high as ten men," Miller said. "You must remember everything I tell you, because you will be telling the same things to everyone who takes the tour."

He pointed around the great, dark room at other supplies of wood, and at some large heaps of dirt that Stephen had not noticed before. "Light two or three fires, so that visitors can see how big the Rotunda is," Miller told him. "If they ask what all this dirt is, and those pipes along the wall, explain that they are old mine diggings left over from the War of 1812. I'll tell you more about that later."

Stephen nodded. He felt a strange emotion, part wonder and part excitement. Although he had spent only a few minutes inside this cave, already he was learning its secrets. He was sure the cave would reveal many more.

Miller picked up his lantern again and led the way through the Rotunda. Now the passage was higher, and much wider than the Narrows. Stephen looked at everything, although it was hard to see very far with only the two lanterns for light.

Miller stopped at the entrance to another passage. "Now here's something important," he told Stephen. "Before you announce the name of this room, you must be sure to tell any ladies that they are not to be alarmed. It is called the Little Bat Room. But there are no bats here in the warmer months, when we get most of our visitors."

Miller held his lantern high. "In wintertime, though, you should see this place. Thousands and thousands of bats, all crowded together, hanging upside down with their wings wrapped tight. They look like little men wearing capes. They sleep all winter long."

Stephen had watched bats flitting above the trees on a summer evening, hunting for bugs to eat. But he'd seen only a few at a time. He tried to imagine what thousands of bats would look like.

"Ladies come into the cave?" he asked Archibald Miller.

"They do indeed," the other man said. "Young ones mainly;

the older ones often can't manage the entrance. You'll see all types of visitors soon."

The Little Bat Room wound deep into the rocky cave. In the dim light, Stephen could see a number of small holes leading into the walls on each side. None was big enough for a person to squeeze inside.

"There's a dangerous pit here at the back wall." Miller stopped and pointed. "You need to keep an eye on your people. Warn them to stay away from it. And make sure you walk in front."

Stephen gripped his lantern. Its shivering flame lit up the left-hand wall. He could see the floor slope down into a place of utmost darkness. Miller picked up a rock and threw it into the hole.

Stephen listened. It seemed a long time before the rock struck bottom. Miller told him, "This is Crevice Pit. It is two hundred and eighty-five feet deep. I know because I measured it myself. Tied a rock onto a rope and lowered it down until the rock struck bottom. Anybody falls in there, they ain't coming out again."

Stephen shivered. He couldn't imagine falling into a hole so dark and deep.

"I always invite people to sit down here and listen to a story." Miller set down his lantern and sat on a chunk of broken rock. "Long before I measured this hole, a fellow went down there on the end of a rope. He was a young slave—even younger than you. The story goes, his boss was looking for peter-dirt. That's one of the makings of gunpowder. They used to dig tons of it out of this cave. Anyway, somebody told the boss the best dirt of all was bound to be at the bottom of a pit, so he lowered a lantern down into that hole to see how deep it went.

"The story goes, the rope broke and he lost the lantern. So he sent this young slave down there. He was hardly more than a boy, so he didn't weigh much. A couple of men tied a good stout rope around him. They lowered him as far as the rope would reach—about forty-five feet.

"That young fellow told the wildest tale when they finally pulled him up. He was shivering and shaking. Swore he'd never go down there again, not for any money. He said that skinny little crevice opens out into an enormous cave room with a huge tunnel in the side. He never found the lamp. Not only that, he claimed he couldn't even see the bottom."

Miller stood up and dusted off his pants. "Nobody believed him. We've never found hide nor hair of any new cave passage. That pit is nothing but a hole in the ground. Now let's get moving. Past this room, the passage comes to an end. We're going back the way we came, to the Church."

Stephen followed obediently, but he was thinking hard. Why couldn't the slave's story be true? Why couldn't there be another level of caverns deep below? He had been in Mammoth Cave only a short while, but he had seen one or two small holes that looked as though they might go somewhere.

Stephen made a promise to himself. One day, he would find out what was at the bottom of Crevice Pit.

The Church and
the Steamboat

THEY RETRACED THEIR steps to the Rotunda. Mr. Miller quizzed Stephen on the names of everything they passed, and made him go in front to show the way. It reminded Stephen of walking in the woods at night. But no nighttime forest was ever as dark as this.

And no forest was ever so quiet. All he could hear was the sound of their breathing and the scuff of their footsteps on the dusty floor.

By now his eyes had adjusted to the low light. He could see his surroundings much better. "This passage ends pretty soon after the Little Bat Room," he recited. "Back up here is the Rotunda." He led the way with his lantern.

Stephen was more fascinated by this cave every minute. It was unlike any other place he had ever known. And his master wanted him to learn all about it! He would be happy to oblige.

He thought of the long summer coming, when the field slaves would have to toil outside even on the hottest days. In the eastern part of Kentucky, hundreds of workers sweated in the hemp fields. Hemp is a plant used to make rope and a rough cloth in which the southern plantation owners wrapped their bales of cotton. It was the most important crop in Kentucky.

Then Stephen thought about himself. His mother always said that God had blessed him with a strong body and a quick mind. White people seemed to look on him with favor. He could have been a carriage driver or a house slave. House slaves mixed with the white masters much more than the field slaves did. That meant they wore better clothing, got better food, and usually had better places to sleep.

But now Stephen had no interest in being a house slave. He felt very lucky to be right where he was. He promised himself that he would become the best guide Mammoth Cave had ever known.

Back in the Rotunda, their little fire was burning down. Archibald Miller stamped it out and led the way across the huge room into another high passageway.

"This is what we call the Grand Gallery," he said. "On the left here are the Cliffs of Kentucky. They're named after the rocky cliffs along the Ohio River. Now, look where I'm pointing. See that hole up there?"

Stephen had to look hard before he located the gap, high up under the cave roof. Mr. Miller said, "You can get through there and climb down the other side, but it's dangerous. Lots of huge rocks, and half of 'em are loose, just lying on each other in a huge pile."

They moved straight ahead down a tall, wide tunnel. Stephen understood why it had been named the Grand Gallery. A gallery is a tall, wide passageway.

They walked for quite a while. Then, suddenly, the tunnel widened into a very large room. Along one wall were rough wooden benches made from split logs. Mr. Miller gestured to Stephen to sit down on one of the logs. Then he held out his hand. "Give me your lantern," he ordered.

Stephen obeyed. Miller took it and began to walk away. What was happening? Was he going to leave Stephen in the dark?

It seemed as though they had been exploring the cave for hours. Stephen could not possibly find his way back alone.

But there was no need for him to worry. As Stephen watched, Mr. Miller climbed up the steep, rocky side of the chamber. He pulled himself onto a ledge and stood up.

Now Stephen could see that someone had built a wooden pulpit up there. It looked just like the one inside the church near Mr. Gorin's house, only not as shiny.

Mr. Miller got behind the pulpit. He flapped his elbows and put his hands on his shirtfront, just like a preacher. Stephen grinned.

Mr. Miller leaned forward to gaze down at Stephen. "In the old days," he said, "there was a preacher who didn't have his own

He flapped his elbows and put his hands on his shirtfront, just like a preacher.

church. Or maybe he did have a church, but he couldn't keep people coming back more than two Sundays in a row. Probably it was because his sermons lasted all day long." He lit his pipe, and Stephen caught the strong smell of tobacco.

Miller went back to his story. "So, he had the bright idea of holding some church services in the cave. First he preached to the slave miners who were working way down here. Then he invited folks to join him on a cave tour, ending with a sermon here in the Church. When he got them here, he had them sit down comfortably, collected all their lanterns, and proceeded to preach at them for the next four hours."

Stephen guessed the ending of the story. "And they couldn't leave because they couldn't find their way out!"

Mr. Miller nodded with approval. He climbed down and gave Stephen's lantern back to him.

Stephen was certainly glad that *he* didn't have to find his own way out. He had no doubt that he could learn these trails, but it was only his first day!

They walked on. This time Stephen spotted something up ahead. It was a wooden ladder, tall but not very strong-looking, leaning against the right-hand wall. At the top was darkness.

"There's a big wide hole up there," said Archibald Miller. "Go on, climb up."

Stephen did as he was told. The ladder was sturdier than it looked. But he was happy to reach the top and climb off onto a wide shelf of rock. The floor seemed a long way down.

Miller came up the ladder, too. He pointed into the entrance.

"This is called the Haunted Chambers," he told Stephen. "When you get up here, set your lantern so that it lights up the ledge. Then go back down and help the customers. Tell them to wait right here until everyone is together."

"Can ladies climb that ladder, Mr. Miller?"

"Most of them choose not to. If you have a lady on the tour, then you either skip this part or ask if she would rather wait below. Never leave her alone, of course. Allow her to stay behind only if others will wait with her. Leave their lanterns with them, and don't take too long away. Now, look over there."

Miller pointed straight across the passageway. Dimly, Stephen could see another opening, about as wide as the one that led into the Haunted Chambers. It was directly across from them at the same height.

"It looks as though this tunnel used to continue on that side, doesn't it?" Miller said. "We investigated that hole, but it chokes up with sand pretty close to the entrance and there's no way to get through."

Again Stephen had the feeling that there was much more of Mammoth Cave waiting to be explored. The cavern seemed riddled with holes. Tunnels up high, pits down low, odd little nooks and crannies everywhere . . . who could say how big Mammoth Cave really was?

Miller was talking. "Let your customers rest a little after the ladder climb. While they're doing that, you can tell them how the Haunted Chambers got its name."

Stephen knew another story was coming. He made himself comfortable on the smooth floor.

"I was telling you about the miners," Miller said. "During the War of 1812 the British Navy blockaded our coastline. Our soldiers were running out of gunpowder because no supply ships could reach Washington. But the man who owned Mammoth discovered that the cave was full of saltpeter. That's the peter-dirt I was telling you about. If you wash down the dirt and mix it with sulphur and charcoal, you get gunpowder.

"My daddy was in charge of the mining operation. He had seventy men digging in here. There were oxen to pull the carts full of dirt, pipes to bring water from the entrance to wash it down, everything they needed. A lot of the work went on right down there." He pointed downward. Stephen could see some old wooden vats. Sticking out of them were wooden pipes leading back toward the cave entrance.

"The workers were all slaves," Miller went on. "One day there was a new man on the job. The overseer asked for somebody to go back into the Salts Room, where there was a lot of good peter-dirt. And although this fellow had been back there only once before, he put up his hand."

Mr. Miller pointed into the Haunted Chambers. "The Salts Room is this way. Come on."

Stephen stood up and followed him. The passage ran straight ahead.

"The fellow knew there were no branch-offs on the way, so he thought he would be fine," Miller went on. "Sure enough, he reached the right place, dug a couple of bags of dirt, and loaded them up to come back to the Grand Gallery. But somewhere along the way, he decided the return trip was taking too long. He got it into his head that he'd taken a wrong turn. Even though there aren't any wrong turns to take, as you can see!"

Miller laughed and shook his head. Stephen didn't think the story was funny. The cave was a strange and peculiar place. Surely a person who had been inside only once before could become confused.

Miller was still chuckling. "The silly fellow dropped his bags and started darting forward, then back again, trying to figure out which way to go. Finally he tripped over a stone and dropped his lantern, and there he was in the dark! Can you imagine?"

Stephen felt sorry for the long-ago slave.

Miller said, "In the meantime, the other fellows are sitting down to have their dinner, when they suddenly realize that he never came back. They decide to put together a search party. But by the time they come upon the lost man, he's completely lost his wits. When he sees them coming, he starts screaming about devils and demons and starts running! They can't catch up with him until he trips over a rock again and falls flat on his face. He told them later he was so scared that he thought he'd been cast into the devil's own region down below."

"And that's why they call these the Haunted Chambers," Stephen concluded.

He still didn't see anything funny about the story. He would remember the tale, and he would repeat it to visitors, but he wouldn't laugh like Mr. Miller had when he did so.

Miller showed Stephen other interesting features of the Haunted Chambers. Here Stephen saw his first stalactites. Miller had him repeat the word several times to make sure he pronounced it right: "stuh-lack-tights."

The stalactites were rock formations that hung down from the roof of the passageway. In other places, the formations grew up from the floor.

"When they grow upward, we call 'em stalagmites." Miller smoothed his hand along one tall growth. "You can remember which one is which because 'stalagmite' has the sound 'guh' in it, like 'ground.' It's the one that grows up from the ground."

Stalagmite, Stephen repeated to himself. *Stalactite.* What interesting words, he thought. Interesting words for interesting things.

This passageway was full of the strange growths. In some places a stalagmite and a stalactite had joined in the middle to form a single column from roof to floor. Many were blackened by the candle smoke of visitors who had come here before. These formations looked almost like the trunks of trees, if trees were made out of rock.

Stephen asked Miller how the stalactites were formed.

"You ask a lot of questions, don't you?" Miller's voice was rough. "Put that one to a scientist."

The tone of his voice made Stephen flinch. Mr. Miller seemed angry at him, and angry men often struck out at slaves. Then Stephen had a thought. Miller probably didn't know the answer to Stephen's question, and he was embarrassed about it. So he was angry at Stephen for asking.

Things were quiet for a moment. Then Miller said, "I believe they were formed by water dripping down from the cave roof. See the way some of them are shaped like icicles? I just don't know why they're made out of rock instead of ice."

He turned back to Stephen. "We'll likely have a scientist or two visiting here this summer," he said. "Why don't you ask one of them? Then you'll know what to answer when somebody asks *you* how they're formed."

Stephen thought that was an excellent idea. He wanted to learn everything he could about the cave.

Miller didn't seem to be a bad fellow. He did not yell at Stephen, like some white men yelled at slaves. Friends of Stephen's had been beaten for working too slowly, or whipped for disobeying. But Archibald Miller simply wanted him to learn.

He showed Stephen how to make one of the biggest stalactites ring like a bell by banging it with a stone. The gonging sounded spooky and hollow in the dark passageway. Next came the Register Room, where earlier travelers had used candles tied onto sticks to burn dates, initials, and even crude drawings onto the roof of the cave. Stephen wondered why people wanted to make dirty smoke marks on such a unique creation of nature.

Miller pointed out the Devil's Arm-Chair, an oddly shaped formation at the bottom of one stalactite, big enough so that visitors could sit down in it and rest. They looked at the Salts Room, where the unlucky slave had worked before getting lost in the tunnel. Then they walked out onto Lovers' Leap, which was a stone ledge projecting out over a dark pit.

Miller held his lantern out over the darkness. Stephen could barely see the bottom of the pit.

"Nobody has ever been so desperate about his ladylove that he decided to jump here," Miller told him. Stephen could understand why. Stalagmites grew up from the ground below like quills on a porcupine's back.

Then he noticed a steep slope at the left edge of the pit. Bootprints showed in the damp earth.

"Yep, that's the way to the lower level," Miller said. "Down there are the Devil's Elbow, a couple of domes and pits, and a spring. But it's a tough trail down. Let's eat first."

They each found a chunk of rock to perch on. Stephen handed the lunch basket to Miller. Now that he was sitting still, Stephen could feel the coolness of the cave air. While he ate, he thought over everything he had seen.

Stone "trees," an underground church, a winter home for

bats, and tunnel upon tunnel upon tunnel. His head felt full of wonderful sights.

The lantern light cast weird shadows around them. The cave air seemed to move, brushing him gently.

Mammoth Cave did not feel like a closed, locked-in place. Stephen had the sense of much more space around him. It could be above his head or deep beneath his feet.

Wherever it was, he would find a way in.

The First Discovery

BY THE END of April 1838, Mammoth Cave was ready for new visitors. Work on the inn was finished, and Archibald Miller was now the manager. At the cave entrance, the wooden handrail made it much safer to descend the rocky stairs. A wooden basin stood beneath the little waterfall so visitors could fill their canteens before entering the cave.

Stephen was ready, too. Miller had shown him all the trails and told him all the stories. Stephen had practiced by guiding some of Mr. Gorin's workmen through the cave as if they were paying customers.

Still, Stephen was nervous. He wanted to do a good job, but what if the visitors didn't like the way he talked about the cave? Would Mr. Gorin replace him with another guide?

April was too early in the year for most travelers to visit the cave. The main stagecoach road went through Bell's Station, about nine miles to the east of the cave. From there, visitors had to come by horseback up a rough trail into the hills. Right now, the road was muddy from spring rains. It was not a quick or easy journey.

So Stephen's first tour was a small one. It was a group of travelers who had decided to stop for two days at the cave during their stagecoach journey from Louisville heading south.

Four men and two women took rooms at the inn. That evening, while Mr. Gorin socialized with the visitors, Archibald Miller called Stephen away from his supper. They met in the yard next to the kitchen. Chickens clucked around their feet.

Miller handed Stephen a bundle.

"This will be your guide uniform," he said. "Wear it whenever you lead a tour, and be sure you keep it clean. If you need something mended or replaced, tell Nita." Nita was the slave woman who cooked at the inn.

Stephen received the bundle with delight. He had never owned a new piece of clothing. As a little child, he had worn nothing but a long shirt that hung down to his knees. Later he made do with cast-off clothing that never seemed to fit and cheaply made shoes that hurt his feet. He wanted to look at the garments right then and there, but Archibald Miller had more to say.

"You will treat every visitor with the deepest respect," the inn manager told him. "They are paying customers. But more than that, they have come a long way to see the cave. It may be the only time they *ever* come. If you do your job well, they will tell their friends and relations all about the tour, and our business will grow."

Stephen bobbed his head. "I will do my best, sir."

He meant it. He felt very lucky to be a guide rather than a field hand, or even a carriage driver or house servant, who were much more respected than slaves who worked outdoors. He did not intend to fail at his job.

In the morning, after breakfast, the visitors were ready for their descent into the cave. Mr. Miller led the chattering group down the hill to the entrance.

Stephen was waiting by the top of the rocky stairs. He wore his new clothing: striped pants, a brown jacket, and a slouch hat. On his feet were the sturdy shoes Mr. Gorin had provided.

Miller introduced him to the travelers.

"This is our boy, Stephen. I trained him myself, and he knows all the trails in the cave. You may feel safe and secure in his presence."

Stephen bowed to the two young ladies. One was tall and strong-looking, the other smaller and more delicate. The smaller woman held the arm of one of the gentlemen.

"I trust you all read the tour rules posted at the inn," Miller went on. "Most important of all is, *do not lose sight of your guide.* If you feel the need to rest, please inform Stephen. The group must stay together at all times. There is no danger in the cave, and no one has ever been injured on a tour. But if you stop, or try to examine something off the trail, it is possible to be left behind by accident."

The ladies whispered to each other. The taller one looked rather excited, but the other was pale.

"Stephen will carry provisions for your visit," Miller went on. He pointed to a large wicker basket covered with cloth. "You will refresh yourself in most unusual surroundings!"

Stephen handed a lantern and a canteen to each of the men on the tour. The taller woman was smiling and seemed ready to go. She twitched her long skirt up to her ankles and proceeded down the rocky stairs.

"Tread carefully, Elizabeth!" the younger woman called. She held back from the steps. "I don't think I am capable of this, Willis," she said to the young man who stood with her.

"I will take perfect care of you. What else is a husband for?" The man gave her a little hug. "Come, Minetta, it will be such fun!"

Archibald Miller said nothing. He glanced at Stephen as if to say, "How can you convince her?"

Stephen thought quickly. He remembered his own first impressions of the cave. Perhaps the lady was afraid of the dark.

"It is most amazing the way one's eyes adjust to the interior of the cave, madam," he said quietly to the woman and her husband, as the others headed down the stairs. "In each large room I build a fire, so that you may see more of the grand surroundings. In the passageways, our lanterns will be quite sufficient to light the way. There is no danger of becoming lost."

The young man looked hopeful. "What do you think, Minetta?" he said. "I do so want to see the cave."

Stephen thought of something else Archibald Miller had told him, about travelers from Europe. "We receive many visitors from the Continent," he said. "They have begun to call this cavern one of the wonders of the world."

The lady smiled, just a little. "Then we must see it, so that we may describe it to our friends in Nashville." She looked at Stephen. "Lead on, guide."

Stephen's heart leaped. He had not lost a customer! Archibald Miller nodded to him and turned to go. Stephen was on his own.

———— • ————

Stephen led many tours in the weeks that followed. As spring turned to summer, the weather grew hot and humid. A steady stream of visitors arrived to spend a few days at the inn, relaxing in the cool shade of the oak and maple trees. And almost every visitor paid to enter the cave.

The hotel provided them with special outfits to cover their better clothing. They were not attractive. But because the tours involved climbing ladders, pushing through dusty passageways, and getting muddy, many people chose to wear the clothing.

On every tour, Stephen began his talk while the visitors filled their canteens. He told them that the temperature inside

Mammoth stayed the same all year round—about fifty-four degrees. His visitors always asked about the curious wind from the cave mouth. Stephen told them that it always blew outward when the outside air was warmer than the air inside the cave. On winter days, when the air inside the cave was warmer than the air outside, the wind blew *into* the cave. His visitors murmured with interest.

Stephen enjoyed answering their many questions. He had taken to carrying his lantern on the end of a long wooden stick so that he could hold it out to light objects a short distance away.

"What are these wooden pipes?" one gentleman inquired, pointing to the ground inside the Narrows.

Stephen explained that the pipes had carried water to the mining operations inside during the War of 1812. He pointed out the ruts left in the passage floor by oxcarts.

"The slaves who worked here left the cave every night, but the oxen could not climb the rocks," he told them. "They stayed inside for months. Yet they lived in perfect health. Farther on I will show you the corncobs still scattered around where the animals used to eat."

The tours seemed to go well. Even visitors who started out being nervous, like the young lady Stephen led on his very first day, enjoyed themselves as they gazed upon the vast Rotunda and the passageways beyond.

And Stephen got very good at telling his stories. He got plenty of practice!

*He had taken to carrying his lantern on the end of a long wooden stick
so that he could hold it out to light objects a short distance away.*

Beyond the Church, Stephen led his tours past an enormous slab of broken stone named Steamboat Rock. One end of this rock came to a point, making it look like a miniature river steamboat without the big paddlewheels.

Steamboat Rock was almost three times as tall as Stephen himself. Behind it was an opening in the cave wall that led to the Wooden Bowl Room. Often Stephen took visitors down the narrow passageway in order to tell them about Mammoth's famous mummy, Fawn Hoof.

"White men were not the first to enter Mammoth Cave," he said to one group, as they followed him down a low tunnel. "Long, long ago, the Indians came inside. Here's how they found their way."

In the Wooden Bowl Room, Stephen showed his customers what the Indians had left behind: short bundles of dried reeds, tied together at one end and burned away at the other. "These are the remains of torches made out of the same cane that grows along Green River today," he said. "The Indians must have burned these to light their way." He showed the visitors other items as well. There were some crude woven mats, a bowl made from a dried-out gourd, and some sticks that were worn on one end, as if they had been used for digging.

And then Stephen told them the story of Fawn Hoof.

"It is unfortunate that you did not visit the cave just a few short years ago," he said. "At that time, you would have seen the famous mummy called Fawn Hoof. Miners digging for saltpeter found her burial place."

The tour customers whispered to each other. The dark cave was a spooky place to be hearing about dead bodies!

Stephen lowered his voice to make the story sound even more mysterious. "They found her mummified body sitting upright in a hole lined with stones," he told the visitors. "She must have been there for a very long time, because her body was all dried out. But she had been buried with loving care. She was wrapped in a deerskin decorated with beads and feathers. Around her neck, on a leather string, hung the hoof of a young deer. And that is how Fawn Hoof received her name."

For a while the mummy was displayed in Mammoth Cave, he told the customers, but later her body was taken away and displayed at curiosity shows around the country.

As the tour moved on, Stephen wondered once again why the Indians came so far into the darkness with only a few flimsy torches for light. What had they been seeking? His customers would talk for a while about the mystery as they followed him out of the Wooden Bowl Room.

A rocky natural staircase leading down from the Wooden Bowl Room was called the Steps of Time. Beyond that was a series of rooms called the Deserted Chambers. Stephen warned the visitors to beware as he showed them Side-Saddle Pit, Covered Pit, and finally, the most frightening chasm of all, Bottomless Pit.

As they approached it, Stephen told his customers to stand still and wait for instructions. Then he held his lantern high. Now they could see that the rocky passageway they were following ended at a steep drop-off. Around the drop-off, walls rose steeply to a high ceiling. Those visitors who were brave enough to creep up to the edge of the drop-off could see no bottom below.

Stephen threw a rock down into Bottomless Pit. The visitors counted while it skipped and clattered down into the darkness. It always took quite a while for the sound to die away, but no one ever heard the rock splash into water below or land on a stony bottom. No one knew how deep the pit really was.

Bottomless Pit was much too wide to jump, and Stephen could see no way down its steep sides. But on the other side of the chasm, the passageway continued. It headed up a gentle slope, then over a rise and out of sight.

Stephen often gazed across the opening, wondering what was on the other side. He had a great urge to explore more of Mammoth Cave. Bottomless Pit was uncrossable for now, but he had another spot in mind.

On Sundays, most slaves were allowed to rest from their labors. Those who wished could attend church and listen to Sunday service from the back of the room. Others cultivated their garden plots or went hunting in the woods. Squirrel, woodchuck, and rabbit made a welcome addition to the bacon, cornmeal, and molasses the slaves were given to eat.

Stephen sometimes went swimming in Green River, which was down the hill from Mammoth Cave. Or he walked the long miles to Glasgow to see his mother and brother. But this Sunday he had a different plan.

He asked Nita for some cornbread and beans for his lunch, filled a lantern with oil, and took plenty of matches. Then, all by himself, he slipped off to the cave.

By now the trails were easy for him. Stephen moved briskly down the Grand Gallery. He kept the lantern light very low, just bright enough that he wouldn't trip over a rock.

He had never been alone in the cave before, but he wasn't afraid. Somehow he felt welcome in that enormous place.

Very soon he reached Steamboat Rock. He passed through the Wooden Bowl Room and the Deserted Chambers. Just before the Bottomless Pit lay the object of his quest. Stephen knelt down beside it, his heart beating fast.

Right here, a crack in the floor led down to a lower level called the Labyrinth. Archibald Miller had taken Stephen this way just once. He had told Stephen that "labyrinth" means a confusing maze. The tunnels on the lower level turned and twisted. It was easy to get lost, and that was why the tours never came this way.

Stephen eased his way down into the narrow opening. He moved carefully. If he dropped the lantern, it might break, and he had no other. It would be a long, dark journey back to the mouth of the cave.

But he felt like a real explorer, and he was determined not to be afraid. He had the feeling that some thrilling sight was just waiting to be discovered. He wanted to be the one to discover it.

He eased down out of the crack and found himself standing in a high, narrow passageway. He tried to remember where Archibald Miller had taken him. In one direction lay Bottomless

Pit, but there was no way to cross it on this level, either. What was in the other direction?

Stephen thought for a moment. He dared not lose his way. Only Nita knew he was in the cave, and she had no idea where he was exploring. If Stephen got lost, no one would know where to find him.

He had tucked a few candles in with his lunch. He dug one out and lit it from the lantern flame. Then he stuck it into a crack between the rocks on the floor and watched to see if it would blow out.

But this deep inside the cave, there was no wind at all. The little flame burned steadily. With it to mark the place where he had entered the Labyrinth, Stephen felt safe to explore further.

He moved down the tunnel cautiously, making sure to watch the floor in front of him. Now the main tunnel began to branch off in many directions. Stephen ventured a little way down one passageway, but quickly returned. All these rocky pathways looked the same. Now he understood why this place was called the Labyrinth.

Then he had an idea.

He lit another candle stub. This time he used the smoke from the candle flame to burn a crude arrow onto the wall of the cave. It pointed back the way he had come.

As long as he marked his way back, he would be safe. He went on, holding his lantern high.

The tunnels twisted and turned, but Stephen kept to as straight a path as he could manage. At each intersection he was careful to smoke an arrow pointing back along his trail.

He came to a place where a dome rose overhead, and remembered that Archibald Miller had shown this to him. Beyond the dome, a steep slope rose up in front of them, and they had decided to turn back.

Now Stephen took another look at this slope. He held his lantern high and walked back and forth. He thought he could see a shadow just under the ceiling. Was there another passageway up above?

Stephen set down his lantern and tried to scramble up the steep slope. The rock was very slippery, and he quickly slid back down. The second time, he looked for handholds and footholds. He climbed partway up, but had to give up when there was nothing else to grab on the smooth wall.

He wouldn't give up. There was another passage up there, he could feel it.

Once again he started up, moving crablike back and forth across the slippery slope. Slowly, slowly, he climbed. The lantern light cast strange wavering shadows on the wall.

This time Stephen was successful. And he was rewarded— for there *was* another passageway ahead of him!

Stephen's lantern still burned down below. He dared not try to climb up here with it; it could easily break. So he pulled out his last candle stub and lit it.

It gave a meager light. Stephen peered into the darkness. He moved forward slowly, making sure that the candle lit the ground ahead of him. There might be cracks or holes in the floor.

Soon he was glad of his caution. He came to a shallow pit. He might have broken his leg if he had walked into it. Then he would have been trapped, maybe to be discovered someday just like Fawn Hoof.

 He slid carefully down into the pit. There was an opening in the right-hand wall, almost like a window. Stephen thrust his candle into the blackness. What he saw made his eyes widen.

He was looking into a huge vertical shaft. It was like looking *up* into a wide, rocky tunnel. Stephen's light was not bright enough to show either a roof or a floor. But straight across from him was a beautiful sight.

Most of the walls in Mammoth Cave were of gray stone. But this shaftway was beautifully colored. It looked as though an enormous yellow-and-white candle had melted down the curved walls. Streaks of red and black added even more color.

Water dripped across the wall from some unseen source overhead. The wet rock gleamed in the dim light from Stephen's candle.

Stephen was thrilled. Was he the first person ever to see this sight? He would not be the last, that was certain. It had not been so difficult to get here from the upper level. Ladders could be built at the steepest parts of the trail so that other visitors could make the journey.

He headed home to tell Mr. Gorin that his cave held a wonderful new tourist attraction.

Across the
Bottomless Pit

FRANKLIN GORIN WANTED to see Stephen's discovery for himself. It had been a long time since anything new was found inside Mammoth. On September 5, 1838, he told Stephen to lead the way back into the cave.

Archibald Miller and George Tapscott, the carpenter, came along as well. Stephen had told them about the slippery climb up the slope, so the men brought a wooden ladder along. They also brought a length of strong rope.

When they reached the Labyrinth, Stephen started forward. Behind him, the others hesitated as they looked at the confusing maze of passages. Then Stephen showed them his arrow markings.

"Very smart, Stephen," Gorin said. He seemed very pleased.

The men carried the ladder to the steep wall that Stephen had worked so hard to climb. Now it was easy to reach the new level. Gorin and the others gazed into the "window" for a look at the new shaft. Archibald Miller had brought some balls of oil-soaked cotton. He lit one and threw it into the pit.

As the burning cotton drifted slowly downward, the glowing flame revealed even more beautiful details of the shaft. Down, down it fell, until it hit a pool of water at the bottom.

"I'd guess sixty, seventy feet deep," Miller said. "And look how high up it goes!"

"It's beautiful. I'm calling it Gorin's Dome," the cave's owner said proudly.

It wasn't fair, Stephen thought to himself. Everyone would believe that Mr. Gorin had made the discovery. There was nothing Stephen could do about it. Mr. Gorin owned the cave. And Mr. Gorin owned *him*. So Stephen kept quiet.

The four men ventured on. They found a second window overlooking the beautiful shaft. Beyond that the passageway seemed to hit a dead end.

Hanging from the roof of the cave was a beautiful stone curtain so wide that it walled off the pathway. The men paused to regard it.

By now Stephen had learned that the stalactites were formed by water dripping down from the surface above the cave. The water dissolved the rock bit by bit. Over hundreds and thousands of years, the dripping water formed stalactites, draperies, and other formations from the dissolved rock.

"Think how long it took to make this," Gorin said, pointing

at the formation blocking their way. "If you ask me, that's been building since the time of Noah's Ark!"

Stephen was moving his lantern up and down, looking closely at the curtain of rock. Now he saw something. Along the left-hand wall, the formation did not reach all the way to the floor!

Stephen got down on his hands and knees. He could see a crack with just enough room to crawl through. "Mr. Gorin," he said, "there's a way through here. I'm going in."

Archibald Miller came, too. The rough stone scraped their shoulders, but they made it past the stone curtain. The passage continued in front of them.

After some grunting and squeezing, the other men joined them. "I had no idea all of this was here," Gorin said. "This cave is more than I bargained for!"

The men made many more discoveries that day. They found several small domes decorated with beautiful orange and white formations. They found a wide passageway with pure white walls and ceiling.

To mark the occasion, Mr. Gorin wrote his name in the cave. He used the smoke from his lantern to make a dark smudge on the rocky ceiling. Then he scratched "F. Gorin, Sept. 5, 1838."

Mr. Gorin wrote something else, too. It was a letter to the newspaper in Louisville, the nearest big city in Kentucky, telling about the new discoveries. After it was published, many more visitors starting coming to the cave.

Stephen was busy. His tours lasted longer now that there were more trails to show. Stairs were built to allow visitors to reach Gorin's Dome. Stephen kept exploring until he knew the new tunnels as well as the old ones. Only the Bottomless Pit stopped him.

One day that fall, Stephen led a group through the cave. One of the men who paid for the tour was H. C. Stevenson, from Georgetown, Kentucky. Stevenson seemed very interested in the cave. Even before they reached the entrance he started asking questions.

Stephen didn't mind. He loved to talk about Mammoth. He showed his customers as much as he could that day, but Stevenson wanted to see even more. The next day, he paid extra for Stephen to lead him on a private tour. He wanted to see things beyond the usual trails.

So Stephen took him to places that were hard to reach. Stevenson was young and healthy and able to squeeze under low ceilings and climb up steep slopes. Stephen showed him a place called the Solitary Cave, which could be reached only by crawling for a long distance. Then the men made their way through the Labyrinth. Stephen held the lantern while his customer viewed Gorin's Dome.

"Like nothing I've ever seen," Stevenson said in admiration. "I'll warrant even the caves in Europe are not so beautiful."

He wanted to see everything, every strange formation and crack in the wall. Stephen was enjoying himself. Stevenson was the first person who seemed as excited as he was about the cave.

Now Stephen took Stevenson to the edge of the Bottomless Pit. Stephen threw down a burning scrap of paper to demonstrate how deep it was. Slowly the paper fell, twisting and turning as it burned, until it was lost in total darkness. No bottom could be seen.

Stevenson whistled. Then he pointed across the pit, to the passageway on the other side. "Have you thought about getting over there?"

All of a sudden, Stephen's stomach felt knotted up. Yes, of course he'd thought about it. But until now there had been nobody to join in his plan.

"I can't do it by myself," he told Stevenson. "But if there are two of us, we could use the ladder."

Ever since stairs were built so that people could reach Gorin's Dome, the ladder Stephen and the others had used was not needed. Stephen dragged it to the edge of the pit. He knew it was long enough to reach across the frightening gap. But he had been afraid that the ladder would slip while he crawled across. With nobody to hold it steady, it might dump him into the darkness.

Stevenson set down his lantern and scratched his head, looking back and forth from the ladder to the opening.

Would this stranger help him? Stephen was breathless. He realized that he had been waiting a long time for this.

"I want to cross, too," Stevenson decided. "I'll hold the ladder for you, then you do the same for me." Stephen nodded eagerly.

They stood the ladder at the edge of Bottomless Pit. Carefully, they lowered it until the other end touched the far side. But as soon as Stephen crawled onto the first rung, the ladder teetered.

Stevenson knelt immediately to brace the ladder. He leaned his weight onto it to hold it down firmly. Stephen could feel the difference.

He and Stevenson looked at each other. Were they crazy to be trying this? Stephen didn't think so. This was the most exciting thing that had ever happened to him. He could see the same excitement in Mr. Stevenson's eyes.

Now Stephen had to figure out how to take his lamp.

Without light, they wouldn't be able to see on the other side. But he needed both hands to hold on to the ladder. How could he take the oil lamp, too?

"I've got an idea," Stevenson said. He reached inside his coat. From his vest pocket he pulled a clean white handkerchief. He wrapped it tightly around the metal handle of the lamp. "Can you carry it in your teeth?" he asked Stephen.

Stephen gave it a try. He gripped the handkerchief wrapped around the handle. At the same time he had to be careful not to let the lamp touch his chest, because it was hot and would burn him. He crawled onto the ladder with the lamp dangling under his chin. It was heavy, and he knew his neck would hurt later. But he didn't care.

Stephen took a deep breath. Then he inched out over the pit.

He did not look down. Instead, he fixed his eyes on the new passageway. He would be the first person ever to set foot in it. Surely the old Indians never got this far.

The ladder rocked very gently as Stephen scooted forward. He moved as quickly as he could. He didn't want to be on this rickety bridge very long!

Closer . . . closer . . . he was there!

He let the lantern clang onto the rocky floor and jumped to his feet. He couldn't help himself. He threw his arms up in the air and yelled.

Stevenson was clapping. "Good work!" he said.

Stephen looked back to see the white man still kneeling in the dirt. Then he turned and looked into the new tunnel. The path rose gently and went over a small hill. Stephen couldn't see any more from where he stood.

"My turn now," said Stevenson. "Hold the ladder."

Stephen remembered that he was on the job. Mr. Stevenson had paid for a private tour. How much farther would he want to go? Stephen would have been happy to explore all day.

Stephen knelt onto his end of the ladder. Stevenson checked very carefully on his side to make sure the legs would stay in place. They would be in deep, deep trouble if their ladder fell into the Bottomless Pit.

Stevenson readied his own lantern and prepared to crawl.

He did not look down. Instead, he fixed his eyes on the new passageway.

Then he made a mistake. He looked down into the pit.

Immediately Stephen could see fear come into the other man's face. Stevenson's forehead was showing beads of sweat, and his hands were shaking on the ladder.

"Mr. Stevenson," Stephen called. Maybe it would help if he kept talking. "I think I hear water down this tunnel. I think we're about to discover something important."

He didn't really hear any water. He just wanted to get Stevenson's attention. But his words worked. Stevenson started moving forward again.

He was soon across. Stephen took his lantern and helped him stand up.

Stevenson passed his hand over his face. "Did it," he said, almost to himself. "What a tale this will make!"

They grinned at each other, two brave explorers. Then Stephen stepped into the new passage and lifted his lantern. They walked forward into the unknown.

Stevenson kept close behind him. The passage was narrow now and headed downhill. The ground underfoot was covered with small pebbles.

Suddenly, they came to a place where the tunnel branched. The main passage headed off to the right. The pathway was wide and high enough to walk comfortably. In front of them, though, the space kept narrowing. The passage sloped very gently up to the ceiling. At the top of the slope was a narrow hole, barely high enough to crawl into.

"What do we do now?" Stevenson asked. He started walking toward the right-hand tunnel.

"Do not lose sight of the guide!" Stephen said quickly. Then he froze. He wanted only to keep Stevenson from running ahead, but it sounded as though he was ordering around a white man. If Stevenson complained to Archibald Miller, Stephen could be whipped.

Stevenson looked sharply at him. But he only held his lantern toward the wide tunnel. "Aren't we going this way?"

The right-hand tunnel would be much easier to explore. But Stephen felt something about the left-hand way. He couldn't even describe what it was. He just knew that he wanted to go in there.

Then Stephen noticed something. The look of the slope heading up into the smaller passage reminded him of something. In the smooth dirt he could see curved patterns just like those in the mud around the edge of a pond. It looked as though water had flowed down from this opening, leaving very fine dirt behind. He explained his thoughts to Stevenson.

"It took a lot of water to bring all this dirt in here," he said. "And look how smooth the walls of that crawlway are. Water came through this opening, for sure."

"Is that important?" Stevenson asked.

Stephen said, "No one has ever found a river in the cave. It would be a huge discovery. Even bigger than crossing the Bottomless Pit."

In the dim light, he could see Stevenson smile. "All right," the white man said. "Lead the way. If you get stuck, I can still back out!"

Stephen crawled up the gentle slope to the hole. He couldn't see far. The passage soon curved out of sight.

"I'll leave my lantern here," Stevenson said. "It's going to be hard enough for you to carry one. Do you really want to do this?"

Stephen did indeed. He had crossed the Bottomless Pit, so why should he stop now? He wanted to see how far they could explore today.

Crouching, he led the way into the passage.

In only a minute his body began to protest. His arm was sore from holding out the lantern. His back was bent so low that finally he had to go on hands and knees. He could hear Stevenson crawling close behind him. The passageway became narrower and narrower, and the smoke from the lamp burned their eyes.

Now he had to stop. The lamp was getting so heavy! He set it down for a minute and pulled his water bottle around from his back.

He could hear Stevenson doing the same. They drank deeply, then rested for a bit. Now Stephen could see that the ceiling ahead was becoming even lower. Could they be heading into a dead end?

Stephen kept his thoughts to himself. Stevenson couldn't see past him, so he had no idea what was coming. Stephen judged that the other man would speak up if he became too worried about the crawl.

He had learned from his job that certain people did not enjoy being inside the cave. Some were frightened of the dark. Others did not like the feel of being underneath so much rock. A few were deathly afraid of low, tight passageways.

But Stevenson seemed to be fine. He even made a small joke as they started crawling again. "I wouldn't want to be a fat man on this trail," he said. "What a misery!"

The smooth dirt floor of the passageway sloped gently upward. Soon Stephen had to lie on his belly, pulling himself by his hands through the winding passageway and pushing along with his feet. Behind him, Stevenson wasn't talking anymore.

Please God, Stephen prayed, *let us reach the end of this passageway*. He dreaded the idea of having to creep out backward along this tight passage.

Then he felt a miracle on his face. It was the slightest breath of air, and it smelled like water.

All this time he had been carefully nudging the lantern along in front of him. Suddenly the lantern tilted forward. Stephen caught it just in time before it tipped over.

They were through! Stephen shouted the good news. Then he gave one last pull on the rocky wall and emerged into a new passageway.

He turned immediately to help Stevenson. But the neatly dressed young man Stephen had guided into the cave that morning was gone. Out of the hole in the wall crawled a man-shaped mass of mud. Even his beard was full of it.

Stephen couldn't help himself. His relief was so great that he suddenly forgot all his slave manners. He burst out laughing at the sight of Stevenson scraping mud off his face.

Stevenson looked up, surprised. His mouth hung open as he gazed at Stephen. Then he looked down at his clothes and realized what he looked like. He pointed at Stephen.

"Did you buy your clothing from the same tailor? For yours looks just the same as mine!" And then he laughed, too.

Stephen wiped uselessly at his pant legs. Even his shoes were filled with mud. But it barely made sense to try and scrape them clean, if they had to go back by the same hole. Instead, he held the lantern out front again.

They had come out into a passage that was easy to walk in. It sloped downhill. This time, the floor was covered with fine sand.

At last he and Stevenson reached a room where several passageways branched off. The lantern light showed them a smooth, muddy floor. Stephen was more and more excited. Maybe all this mud meant they were about to reach some large body of water.

Stephen had an idea. He pointed to the damp ground. "If you walk there, your footsteps will be the first since Creation," he told Stevenson, and handed him the lantern. "Go ahead!"

Stevenson did so. He left a trail of footprints to the opposite wall. Then he lifted the lantern and peered down the nearest tunnel. "Come on!" he commanded.

The two men were powerfully excited. There were new tunnels on all sides. Stevenson would be leaving Mammoth Cave soon, but Stephen had many days of exploring in front of him.

At last, just as they were both getting tired, Stephen and his customer reached the edge of a cliff. Far below them, down a slippery slope, they could see water. The lantern light dimly showed them a stream of water, flowing out of sight in both directions.

This time it was Stevenson who gave a whoop of glee. "Ya-hooooo!" he yelled as loud as he could. The echoes lasted for a long time. Stephen was just as excited. If a bridge was built across Bottomless Pit, and if the tunnel he and Stevenson had squeezed through could be dug out to create an easier passage, visitors would have many new sights to behold in the cave.

Stevenson was gazing down at the dark, silent stream below them. "Let's call it the River Styx," he said.

The River Sticks? That couldn't be right. "What does it mean?" Stephen asked. So Stevenson told him the old Greek myth while they rested from their travels.

"The Styx marked the boundary of the underworld," Stevenson said. "The ancient Greeks believed that when a person died, his spirit traveled far below ground, to the shores of the River Styx. The only way to cross to Hades, the land of the dead, was on a ferryboat. But the boatman would not take you there without payment. Any dead spirit who couldn't give him a coin was left on shore, doomed to wander forever. That's why when a Greek person died, he was buried with a coin under his tongue to pay the ferryman."

Stephen looked down at the river again. "I thank God I'm alive, then," he said. "For I haven't a penny to pay with."

Stevenson laughed. "I'll give you more than a penny when we get back. This trip is worth a gold piece!"

A New Master

H. C. STEVENSON KEPT his word. When they returned to the hotel, he told Franklin Gorin he'd had the most exciting day of his life. He couldn't stop talking about his adventures. He praised Stephen and handed him a piece of gold.

Stephen looked quickly at Mr. Gorin. Under the Kentucky slave code, his master could take the money. Many owners hired out their slaves but kept the earnings for themselves.

But Franklin Gorin was smiling widely. "First Gorin's Dome, now across the Bottomless Pit," he said. "I'll have to write another letter to the papers! You've earned your dollar, Stephen."

A few weeks later Mr. Gorin called to Stephen from the back door of the hotel. Stephen hurried over. Gorin was holding a newspaper.

"Look, here's my letter," he said, and pointed to the second page of the *Louisville Journal.* He read it aloud to Stephen. It was about how H. C. Stevenson, in the company of a guide, had crossed the Bottomless Pit for the first time in history. It told of Stevenson's discovery of the River Styx, the first river ever found in the cave.

"Now the cave will be even more famous," Mr. Gorin told Stephen. He was beaming with pride.

Stephen smiled, but inside he felt angry. The letter had not described what had truly happened in the cave. Anyone who read the newspaper would think that H.C. Stevenson had been the first one to cross the Bottomless Pit and reach the River Styx. Stephen was not even mentioned by name!

The man he had guided could never have made it across the pit by himself. It had been Stephen's idea to use the ladder, and he had told his friends all about the adventure. They knew the truth—but no one else would.

Even thinking about the dollar he had earned didn't help. He would never feel the same about that day.

But there was no time for Stephen to mope around. The next few weeks were busier than ever before, as visitors from Louisville and other Kentucky towns came to see the cave. Even so, Stephen found time to explore. As the weeks passed, he found more and more new passageways. He also helped build a sturdy wooden bridge across the Bottomless Pit so that visitors could be conducted across it in safety.

Stephen was working very hard. All slaves worked long days, from sunup to sundown, but they were allowed a few hours' rest during the hottest part of the afternoon. Underground in the cave, Stephen was away from the broiling sun, so he did not receive a midday break. Those who came to the cave wanted to see everything they could. As a result of Stephen's many new discoveries, the tours sometimes lasted for twelve hours!

Stephen was becoming exhausted. One day Franklin Gorin told Stephen that he was renting two slaves from a man in Nashville, Tennessee. They were named Mat and Nick Bransford. Stephen would train them, and they would work as guides, too. That way Stephen would have some time to rest—and more time for exploration. Mr. Gorin was hoping for more great discoveries.

Nick and Mat were about the same age as Stephen, and the three had a good time together as the new men learned how to be guides. Stephen thought it felt odd to be a teacher, but he always enjoyed talking about the cave. Soon Nick and Mat were ready to lead tours on their own.

One of the people Stephen took on a tour around that time was named John Croghan. He was a medical doctor who lived in Louisville, about ninety miles north of Mammoth Cave.

Croghan visited the cave several times. Stephen noticed that he paid close attention to everything. He even carried a pencil and a little leather-bound notebook with him. He asked Stephen many questions.

One night Stephen saw Dr. Croghan talking with Franklin Gorin. They were walking around the outside of the inn, and the doctor was pointing at things as they talked.

The next morning, Mr. Gorin called all the workers together. He had an odd look on his face. "I have an announcement to make," he said. "I have decided that the cave needs a new owner. Dr. John Croghan has convinced me that he can make Mammoth a major attraction, the likes of Niagara Falls. He will build a new hotel and make many other improvements."

Stephen and the other slaves were silent. But Archibald Miller and some of the other white men were asking questions loudly. Mr. Gorin raised his hands for silence.

"Your jobs are safe. You may stay with the cave. Stephen, Nita, all of you . . . Dr. Croghan is your new master. He has promised me that you will continue here. No one will be sent away. God bless you. I will miss you all."

He turned away quickly. Then Dr. Croghan stepped to the front of the group. His clothing was well made, and Stephen noticed that he carried a gold pocket watch. He looked as though he was a wealthy man.

"Let me tell you how I heard about Mammoth Cave," he said to the assembled workers. "I studied medicine in Scotland. While traveling in Europe I met some people who had toured Mammoth during their visit to our country. They said that the cave was as grand a wonder as Niagara Falls. And they were amazed that I had never been here. Finally, I came to see for myself."

He swept his arm across the inn yard. "I am going to build

a brand-new hotel, with rooms and services to please the finest gentry. We will improve the road so that coaches can drive right to the door. Stephen, that passage to the river you found—we're going to dig out the mud so people can get through more easily."

Dr. Croghan paused for a moment. Then he said to all his listeners, "You are here at a marvelous time for Mammoth Cave. I am pleased to be its new owner."

And that was that. Stephen and the other slaves had a new master. Archibald Miller had a new boss. Later Mr. Miller told Stephen that Franklin Gorin had sold the cave, the inn, and all the slaves for $10,000. "I don't think he would have sold if he'd had the money for improvements," Miller said. "So maybe we're better off with the doctor. He seems to have plenty to spend."

And spend he did. Dr. Croghan ordered a new two-story hotel to be built, much fancier than the old inn. New workers and slaves were brought in. Dr. Croghan got the state of Kentucky to pay for improved roads so that stagecoaches would be able to reach the cave more easily. More and more visitors arrived. But with Mat and Nick helping to lead the tours, Stephen still found time to explore.

There were so many passageways down in the darkness! Across the Bottomless Pit were many new trails and chambers. Every discovery needed a name. The narrow passage to the river became Winding Way, and later was renamed Fat Man's Misery. A broad, arched tunnel became Pensico Avenue. Another of Stephen's finds was called the Bacon Chamber. Flowing water had carved strange shapes in the ceiling that looked like big slabs of raw bacon.

Stephen became very interested in how the cave had been formed. Many of the wider avenues looked like dried-up river-beds, with curving walls and rounded ceilings. Others passage-ways were more like cracks or splits in the rock. Many scientists visited the cave, and Stephen asked them questions. One visitor gave him a book on geology, the study of the earth.

Stephen was delighted, even though he barely knew his letters. In most of the slave states it was illegal to teach a slave to read. Kentucky was one of only three that did not have such a law. But books were expensive, and nobody felt it was impor-tant to educate slaves. Stephen spent many hours puzzling out the scientific words in the book. He was determined to learn.

When he finished that first book, he asked Archibald Miller to lend him some others. He remembered H. C. Stevenson's story about the River Styx, and asked for a book about the Greek myths. And he asked for more about geology.

He also read newspapers that were left behind in the inn. Here Stephen learned what was going on in big cities like New York, Philadelphia, and Washington, D.C.

The news from Washington, the nation's capitol, was espe-cially interesting. Late at night, in his cabin, Stephen would read aloud by lamplight to some of the other slaves.

In the year 1836, Arkansas had joined the country as a slave state. In 1837, Michigan joined, too, as a free state. Now there was thirteen of each, free and slave.

The newspapers talked endlessly about what might happen when more territories wanted to become part of the United States. Should the people living there be allowed to own slaves?

Stephen read aloud some of the arguments raging in Washington, D.C. Senators and representatives from the slave states argued loud and long that no one could be forced to give up his slaves. Slaves were property just like horses and farms. If people moved to new territories and took their slaves along, no Northerner was going to pass a law saying they couldn't keep them there.

The Northern states argued just as loudly that owning slaves was wrong. Although Northerners had owned slaves, too, back in the early days of the country, all of the Northern states had passed laws against slavery by now. Many free blacks lived and worked in Cincinnati, Buffalo, and other big Northern cities.

But in the South, the white men who were getting rich by growing cotton and sugarcane needed thousands of slaves to do the backbreaking work. If slavery was abolished, who would pick all the cotton, chop the sweet sugarcane, care for the farm animals and buildings, cook for the masters, and do all the other hard work? The plantation owners said they couldn't afford to pay workers to handle all the jobs the slaves did. They absolutely refused to let their people go.

Stephen and the other slaves talked quietly about the debates going on in Washington. They were careful not to let anyone overhear them. Dr. Croghan seemed to be a reasonable master, but if anyone heard them talking about freedom, they might not be allowed to gather together. And slaves who rose up against their owners in Kentucky could be hanged.

Stephen did not have too much time for reading, but he worked hard at it. He realized that if he wanted to become a real expert on Mammoth Cave, he would need to know more about it than anyone else around did.

Beyond the River Styx, Stephen found another long hallway. And beyond that, another river. This one was in an underground tunnel that gave a wonderful echo. It became known as Echo River. Stephen wondered whether it led to the outside. He spent many hours exploring up and down the water.

One day while Stephen was resting along the bank of Echo River, he thought he saw something in the water. He bent closer. It wasn't his imagination. There were fish down there! Tiny ones, only a few inches long. He'd never seen fish in the River Styx.

Stephen had learned how to grabble—catch fish with his bare hands—when he was a child. Now he laid his hat upside down beside him and waited. When two of the little fish swam within reach, he grabbed.

Got one! Stephen cupped the wiggling creature in his hands. He dropped it into his hat and looked closer.

What was this! This fish had no eyes!

Were all the river fish blind? Or did he just happen to catch

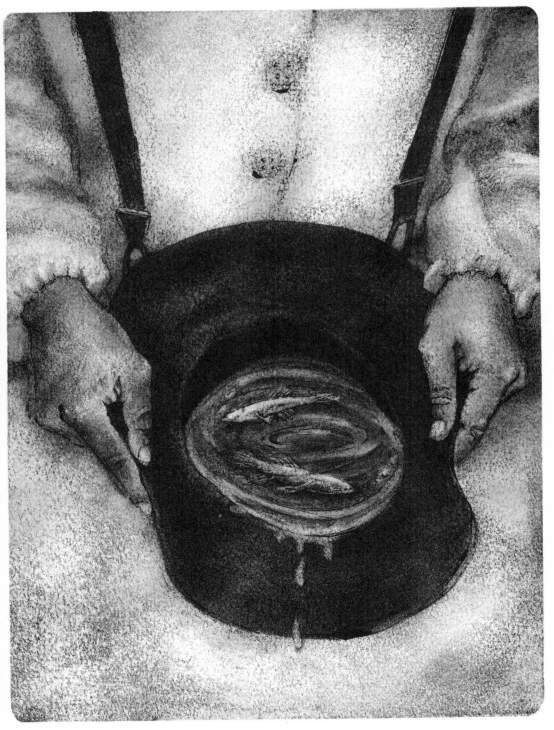

What was this! This fish had no eyes!

a strange one? He tried for another fish, missed it. He splashed water into his hat, hoping to keep the first one alive. Then he tried again for another fish, and caught one this time.

This fish was eyeless, too!

Stephen had never seen anything so strange. He was glad the little white fish was so tiny. If it had been big, he would have been frightened to look at its eyeless face. There was no sign of any eye socket. Just smooth rows of scales where eyes should be.

Visiting scientists had often asked him whether animals lived in the cave. Until now, Stephen had seen nothing but bats and a few beetles, rats, and spiders that lived near the entrance and spent only part of their time in the cave. He knew that scientists would be fascinated by these bizarre fish.

Stephen didn't hesitate. He opened his water bottle and gently slid the two fish in. Then he filled the bottle to the top with river water. He'd go thirsty on the way back, but it would be worth it.

Under Crevice Pit

DR. CROGHAN WAS in the new hotel when Stephen arrived at the back door. The doctor ordered Nita to bring him the
fancy tureen that she used for serving soup. Then he emptied
Stephen's water bottle into the big glass bowl. The fish were
still alive. Dr. Croghan leaned over them, marveling.

Newspaper stories quickly followed. Blind cave fish discovered at Mammoth Cave! New species of fish never before
encountered! Found only in Echo River, deep within the cave!

Mammoth Cave became a must-see attraction for travelers.
Its fame had started to grow with the discovery of Gorin's Dome.
Stephen's crossing of the Bottomless Pit made it even more fam-
ous. Now visitors came by the coachload.

Some of them were scientists who studied animals. Stephen
was asked to grabble for the blind fish again and again. In return,
he asked the scientists questions. Why didn't the fish have any

eyes? Was it because there was nothing to see? There was never any sunlight deep in the cave. So maybe they didn't need eyes. But then how did they find their food?

Stephen loved to show new visitors around the cave. Sometimes he pretended that he was a gracious host showing visitors around a marvelous dwelling. Proudly he pointed out the massive rooms, the gaping pits in the floor, the beautiful formations left by dripping water.

But Stephen enjoyed his time alone in the cave best of all. When he was exploring, there was no one to tell him what to do. He was his own master—for a few short hours at least.

It had been about two years since Stephen started exploring the cave. Even after all his discoveries so far, he believed there was much, much more to be found in Mammoth. Sometimes as he sat beside Echo River, he could feel a tiny breeze touch his skin. Where was the fresh air coming from? Did the river open to the outside somewhere that he could find?

Stephen learned about some caves in Europe from a scientist who took his tour. In the 1700s, an adventurer was exploring a cave called Adelsberg. He discovered an underground lake, but he could not tell how big it was because there was no way to walk around it. So he invented a clever way to light up the darkness.

"He brought two large geese underground with him," the scientist told Stephen. "He harnessed each of them to a tiny wooden boat and set candles on the boats. Then he scared the geese away from the shore. As they paddled about, he was able to see much more of the lake and the cave walls surrounding it."

But in the United States, no one before Stephen had done much cave exploring. Stephen had to invent methods of finding his way into the darkness and back again.

He taught himself safe ways to enter unexplored passages. If a crack seemed too tight, he made sure Mat or Nick waited outside, ready to pull him out if he got stuck. He never slid *down* a slope unless he was sure he could climb back *up*. His climbing ropes wore out quickly against rocky ledges and slopes, so he frequently asked for new ones. Stephen also stuffed padding into his cap to protect his head from falling stones and jutting rocks.

Stephen had a very good memory. He could remember every hole he struggled through and every strange formation he passed. He always marked his trail, but many times he didn't really need the markings to find his way back.

Dr. Croghan had workers build a shallow boat wide enough to carry eight people at once. The workers followed Stephen deep into the cave. They tied the boat at the edge of Echo River. Now Stephen and the other guides could take visitors on a boat trip down the silent, black stream.

Stephen loved this part of the tour. First he would tell his travelers to remain perfectly quiet and still, so that the only sound was Stephen's paddle dipping in the water.

Then he would begin to sing. The cave magnified his voice and made it sound as though two or three men were singing all at once. Stephen's favorite song was one his mother had taught him.

Wade in the water,
Wade in the water, children,
Wade in the water,
God's gonna trouble the water.

The slaves sang many songs that had to do with freedom, and this was one of them. Most of the visitors did not realize that he was singing about the end of slavery, though. They just enjoyed the beautiful tune.

Then Stephen would invite the people on his tour to make their own noises. The ladies clapped their hands and laughed at the sound of the echoes. One gentleman borrowed Stephen's paddle and slapped it on the water. Others whistled. And on one tour, a man pulled out his pistol and shot it!

The noise was tremendous. All the ladies screamed. Stephen was so surprised, he almost fell out of the boat. The shot echoed over and over. It took a long time to die out.

Stephen noticed that the water in Echo River rose whenever the weather was rainy. He also noticed that Green River—the river outside the cave—would rise at exactly the same times. Were the two rivers connected?

He kept on exploring. Sometimes he would find a new passageway high up a wall, just under the ceiling. Other times he

The shot echoed over and over.

would see a crack that was filled with loose rocks. Something would tell him that there was a new tunnel there. He would spend hours pulling rocks out of the hole—and many times his instincts were right. The crack would get wider and he would be able to push his way into yet another new room or tunnel.

One day in the year 1840, a paying customer from Germany asked Stephen to show him part of the cave that nobody else had visited before. Stephen knew exactly where to go. He took the visitor to River Hall. Then they climbed the sandy slope up the right-hand wall and entered a long stoopway too low for them to walk upright. At the end of the stoopway, they found a collapse of rocks.

Stephen began enlarging the passage so they could get through, passing rocks back to the visitor. It was hard work. Most tourists would have complained and asked to go some-where else, but Stephen had judged that this particular visitor would help him.

They dug for a long time. At last, they broke through onto a flat area. In front of them the flat area ended. Darkness lay below.

Both men raised their lanterns high. An amazing sight met their eyes!

They stood on a ledge alongside an enormous pit. Straight across were majestic columns that looked as though they belonged in a temple. The walls were covered with beautiful cream-colored flowstone—formations that looked like draperies, formed by dripping water. The dome was so high overhead that it was lost in the shadows.

The two men were thrilled. They had made an enormous discovery. This was the largest room Stephen had ever found, and it was truly beautiful. And he had a feeling that high overhead was the answer to a riddle he had been wondering about for two years.

Stephen had a very good sense of where he was in the cave at all times—a good "mental map." Right now he was sure he was standing far below Crevice Pit, the one Archibald Miller had showed him on his first day in the cave. Stephen remembered Miller's story about a young slave who was lowered into Crevice Pit on the end of a rope. The slave had reported an enormous, beautiful cave down below—but nobody had believed him.

That long-ago slave was probably dead by now. But Stephen would make sure the guides changed their story about Crevice Pit. All he had to do was get someone to lower a lantern while he waited here below. If he could see the light coming, he would have his proof.

The gigantic shaft became known as Mammoth Dome. It is one of the most spectacular sights in the cave. And it does indeed connect to Crevice Pit. On Stephen's second trip there, he reached the very bottom of the dome. There he found a broken oil lamp—the one dropped by the miners so many years ago.

The Underground
Hospital

IN THE YEAR 1842, a terrible disease was killing thousands upon thousands of people across the twenty-six states and the western territories. In those days it was called consumption. Today we know it as tuberculosis, or TB.

It struck the young, the middle-aged, and the old. The first signs of illness were fever and sweats, mostly in the evening and at night. The sufferers felt weak. Then their chests began to hurt. This was because the disease was attacking their lungs.

As the sickness progressed, patients began to cough all the time. When they started to cough up blood, their relatives knew it was time to choose a gravestone—the patients were going to die.

Doctors didn't know how to treat consumption. They tried many experiments in hopes of finding a cure. But in the year 1842, consumption was still killing more people in the United States than any other disease was.

In his clinic in Louisville, Kentucky, Dr. Croghan had many patients suffering from consumption. He tried to help them, but nothing worked. Then one day he had an idea.

Doctors had noticed that most people who suffered from consumption lived in cities. Not so many people caught the disease out in the countryside. And sometimes patients who left their city homes and went to a hospital away from crowds and noise got better.

Maybe bringing his patients to Mammoth Cave would help them improve, Dr. Croghan thought. He believed that the air inside the cave was clean and pure. The temperature was always the same, and maybe that would help the patients, too. He would set up a hospital inside the cave!

John Croghan asked his Louisville patients whether they would like to join his experiment. A few of the patients had visited the cave, and the others had heard about it. All of them were frightened about having consumption, because they knew they were likely to die.

So several of them agreed to give the idea a try. But the sick people would need a place to stay. Dr. Croghan ordered his slaves to build several cottages deep inside the cave.

Just beyond Steamboat Rock, the cottages went up. The first two were constructed out of stones collected from inside the cave. They had tiny square windows and roofs made of canvas. Slaves brought in beds, storage chests, benches, and other items to make the patients comfortable.

Stephen watched the cottages being built as he led tours past the Grand Curve and on down the tunnel toward the Cataracts. He didn't know what to think. He had heard that the patients would live in the cave day and night until they got better.

Stephen didn't think he would like to spend every minute inside Mammoth, even if he did have a bad disease. He was always happy to come out into the sunlight or into a moonlit evening. In the cave there were no trees, no grass, no flowers. No sun shone, no birds sang. He wondered how the consumption patients would adjust to such a strange life.

The first patient to arrive was a doctor himself. In the summer of 1842, Dr. William Mitchell came to Mammoth Cave from Glasgow, Kentucky. He spent five weeks in one of the stone cottages and then left, pronouncing himself "very much relieved."

The experiment seemed to be a success! Other doctors heard the news and asked if they could send patients to the cave. Men and women arrived from New York, Pennsylvania, Alabama, and South Carolina. New wooden huts had to be built to house them all.

Now when Stephen took a tour past the hospital, he would see a very strange sight. Patients wandered among the huts. They were afraid to go far for fear of getting lost. A few feeble lanterns shed some light in each cottage, but it was very dark everywhere else. Potted plants lined the pathway. They soon withered from lack of sunlight.

At mealtime, a couple of slaves brought provisions from the

inn. One of them was Stephen's friend Alfred. Part of Alfred's job was to climb onto a rock and blow a horn to announce that the food had arrived.

Stephen was there one day to see what happened next.

Patients dressed in long white robes drifted out of the huts like ghosts floating across the rocky floor. Several coughed into handkerchiefs. They had all grown thin and pale during their time in the cave.

Stephen knew the patients had almost nothing to do all day. Many did not feel well and spent hours in bed. Others tried to talk to the visitors who passed through, but no one wanted to get very close to them. They were afraid they would catch consumption, too.

Several times Stephen guided friends or relations down to see the patients. The visitors stopped at the cottages while he led other paying customers farther along the trail. On the way back he would collect them and take them back to the mouth of the cave.

One night Stephen was sound asleep when a knock came at the door of his cabin. Stephen pulled on his pants and went to the door. Another slave was standing there. "Master wants you," he said.

Doctor Croghan was waiting nearby. In the light from his lantern he looked very tired, as if he had not slept. "Come, Stephen. You need to lead a party into the cave."

In the middle of the night? It would make no difference inside the cave, since it was always dark there. But this request was very odd.

*Patients dressed in long white robes drifted out of the huts
like ghosts floating across the rocky floor.*

Stephen got his shirt and jacket and followed the doctor into the chilly winter air. "What has happened, sir?"

Dr. Croghan's shoulders were slumped.

"One of my consumption patients has died. I want to remove him from the cave as quickly as possible for burial."

Stephen shivered, and not just because of the cold. The slaves loved to tell ghost stories. Stephen had never seen anything that looked like a ghost, even in the darkest corners of the cave. But he hoped the sick man had died quietly and that his soul had found its way back outside.

A small group of slaves was waiting with a makeshift stretcher. Croghan's medical assistant was there, too, looking tired and nervous. In the rustling darkness, the party proceeded toward the cave.

The nighttime journey went smoothly. But it would not be the last time Stephen helped with such a task.

Dr. Croghan's experiment turned out to be a failure. Most of his patients were already very sick when they arrived, and not a single one got better.

In all, five men and women died in the cave. One by one their bodies were laid out on a wide slab next to one of the stone cottages. The place became known as Corpse Rock.

The rest of the patients all decided to leave. The experiment lasted only a few months. Then the tunnels were empty again. By the spring of 1843, only the two stone cottages and Corpse Rock remained.

Stephen Draws a Map

BY NOW STEPHEN, Mat, and Nick had discovered so many new passages, pits, and other features that the old maps of Mammoth Cave were hopelessly out of date. All of them stopped at Bottomless Pit. A new map was desperately needed.

In the winter, very few visitors came down Green River or rode the stage over the bumpy track to Mammoth Cave. The hotel stayed open, but most of the rooms were empty. The guides did not have much to do.

Stephen would have been happy to keep exploring, but his master had another idea.

Dr. Croghan wanted to publish a book about the cave. It would have stories about the cave, descriptions of the wonderful sights there, and drawings of some of the most famous features. He planned to have the book printed at his own expense and to sell it in the United States and in Europe. If it was a good book, it would make many more people interested in visiting Mammoth Cave.

Dr. Croghan paid two artists to draw views of the most interesting parts of the cave: Bottomless Pit, the river scenery, the great domes with their beautiful flowstone walls. The new book would also need a new map. Who better to draw one than Stephen? He knew more miles of the cave than anyone else did.

In the winter of 1842, Dr. Croghan took Stephen home with him to Locust Grove, his farm outside Louisville. He lodged Stephen in a small room next to the kitchens, which were in a separate building out back. Although Stephen was only a slave, Dr. Croghan gave him a place to work inside the big house, furnished with a desk and a lamp.

Stephen was very comfortable at Locust Grove. He slept warmly at night, and he made friends with the other slaves. He started to draw the map his master wanted.

For many days Stephen labored with a large sheet of paper and a sharp pencil. He started by tracing a map that had been drawn in 1835. It showed only the old avenues, nothing beyond the Bottomless Pit. Then he started to add on the many new miles that had been discovered since 1838.

He drew the biggest passageways first. In his mind he followed the trails he had walked so many times, remembering where each one curved or widened or came to a dead end.

Sometimes one of the other slaves brought Stephen a meal;

In his mind he followed the trails he had walked so many times,
remembering where each one curved or widened or came to a dead end.

other times Stephen joined the kitchen workers for supper. Every evening Dr. Croghan asked him how the map was coming along.

"It is an enormous job, sir," Stephen told him. Dr. Croghan had invited him into the cozy sitting room, where there was a fire burning. Outside it was dark and a few flakes of snow were beginning to fall.

"If you need any aid, just tell me," Croghan said. "I can bring Mat or Nick to help, if you cannot remember all the trails."

Stephen just smiled. He remembered the trails. It was just that there were so many, it was taking a long time to draw them!

Dr. Croghan's study was full of books. Stephen had never seen so many. The doctor saw him looking at the leather-bound volumes. "Do you read, Stephen?" he asked.

"I do," replied Stephen, "but I have very little to practice with."

"You may choose something to read while you're at Locust Grove," the doctor said. "Here are biographies, these are essays, I have a Bible...."

"Do you have anything about caves?" Stephen was excited. He had been wanting to read about caves in other places.

Dr. Croghan smiled. "Certainly I do! Let me look...." He stood up and went to the bookshelf. Soon he pulled down a handsome volume with gold lettering on the front.

"This is a book about traveling in Europe. There are excellent descriptions of the major caves." Then he pointed to another area of the shelf. "Here are several books on geology. They talk about the different types of rock, and the way landscapes are formed. I find it a fascinating study."

Stephen left with five precious books cradled in his arms. He couldn't wait to start reading.

It was just before Christmas, and Dr. Croghan's relations were visiting at Locust Grove. His brother, George, was there with his daughters, Serena and Angelica. There was a room in the cave named after each of them. Serena's Arbor was a charming little room at the far end of Cleaveland Avenue. Angelica's Grotto was found in Pensico Avenue.

With so many people in the house, the slaves were kept busy. But Christmas was special. The kitchen workers were given a chicken to roast for their dinner. The women baked biscuits instead of the corn bread they usually ate, and they cooked many different vegetables, like snap beans and greens. And each slave received a treat from Dr. Croghan—an orange and a stick of peppermint candy. It was a real celebration.

When dinnertime came, Stephen's piece of chicken had the wishbone in it. One of the little boys noticed and jumped up. "Stephen's got the pully-bone! I want one end!" Stephen let him hold one end of the wishbone. Then they both pulled.

"I got the big end! I get a wish!" the little boy said. Stephen knew what he would do with his piece.

The slaves always said that if you put the short end of the pully-bone over your doorway, you would meet the person you were going to marry. Stephen looked around the kitchen. All the women there already had husbands, or they were still little girls. He didn't see how the old story could work this time, but he kept the little piece of bone anyway.

Late that night, after everyone had gone to bed, Stephen carefully set the pully-bone on the ledge over his doorway. Then he said his prayers and went to sleep.

The next morning, he was still in his room when someone knocked at the door. "Come in," said Stephen. He was expecting the little girl who brought him a bowl of water to wash with.

But when the door opened, there stood a young woman he had never seen before. She smiled as she set the water down on Stephen's table. "Good morning," she said.

"Who are you?" Stephen asked. She was a very pretty girl, with shining brown eyes and bright red lips. Stephen couldn't help but remember the pully-bone over his doorway.

"My name is Charlotte," said the girl. "And you're Stephen. Miss Tilly told me." Tilly was the head cook for Dr. Croghan's household.

"Where have you been since I got here?" asked Stephen.

"With my mama. She's been sick. Dr. Croghan let me visit with her for a while." Charlotte looked sad. "She's still not better. Now my sister is with her."

Stephen reached out his hand to comfort her. Charlotte

81

touched it for just a second, then she turned back to the door. "I have to do my work now. I'll see you at suppertime!" She smiled and left.

Stephen had to start work himself. The map was going well, although there were still many trails to draw. But for the first time, Stephen found it hard to concentrate. Suddenly there was something other than Mammoth Cave to think about.

Charlotte and Stephen became close friends. Charlotte was one of the house slaves at Locust Grove. Her job was to clean the bed chambers, make sure Dr. Croghan's clothing was well taken care of, and help the doctor's housekeeper in many other ways.

The map took twelve days for Stephen to finish. Then Dr. Croghan's brother George took over. His job was to add labels to the major features, like the Bottomless Pit and Mammoth Dome. He also drew over Stephen's pencil lines with a fine ink pen. Then the map was ready for the printer.

Stephen knew he would not be staying at Locust Grove. Now that the map was finished, he would be sent back to the cave. The journey was long, more than ninety miles. How would he be able to see Charlotte again?

Then he had an idea. The hotel at Mammoth Cave was a busy place during most of the year. Maybe there was some work that Charlotte could do there. Would she want to leave Locust Grove? Would Dr. Croghan allow her to? Slaves could not just choose their own jobs and places to live.

First he spoke to Charlotte. He told her that he didn't want to be away from her. Did she feel the same way about him?

Charlotte looked down into her lap. They were sitting in Stephen's room. She was quiet for a moment, but then she looked up and gave him a beautiful smile. Her answer was yes.

Dr. Croghan was getting ready to return to his patients in Louisville. The Christmas season was over, and it was time for everyone to go back to work. The night before the doctor left, Stephen asked if he could speak to him about Charlotte.

Stephen knew he was making a big request. But he thought Dr. Croghan would take him seriously. Because of Stephen's discoveries, Mammoth Cave was receiving more visitors than ever before. Dr. Croghan had made a lot of money. He should want Stephen to be happy.

First Stephen returned the books that the doctor had loaned him. Then he made his request about Charlotte.

Dr. Croghan listened carefully. "Charlotte is a good girl and a hard worker. We would be sorry to let her go from Locust Grove," he said slowly. He looked straight at Stephen. "Do you love her? Do you want to marry her?"

Stephen thought very hard before he answered. He liked Charlotte very much, he told Dr. Croghan, but they had only met a few days ago. If she worked at the Mammoth Cave Hotel, they would have a chance to know each other better.

Dr. Croghan nodded slowly. "I see. Let me think about it. I'll speak to you in the morning."

Stephen barely slept all night. In the morning, he had his answer. Charlotte would stay at Locust Grove until spring, when the stagecoaches would start bringing visitors to the cave. Then she would come to work at the hotel as a chambermaid.

Stephen and Charlotte were overjoyed. They said thank you again and again. Dr. Croghan smiled and climbed into his carriage, heading back to Louisville.

Charlotte did indeed come to the Mammoth Cave Hotel, and soon she and Stephen "jumped the broom," as it was called when two slaves became man and wife. A slave preacher was there to oversee the marriage. Dr. Croghan even paid for a big party.

Stephen took Charlotte into the cave one day, just the two of them. He took her over the bridge across Bottomless Pit, then down a side passage that few visitors traveled. There he let his lantern smoke smudge the underside of an overhanging rock. When the rock was blackened, he scratched the shape of a heart and inside it the words, "Stephen L. Bishop, Guide, M. Cave. Mrs. Charlotte Bishop, 1843." Outside the heart he wrote: "Mrs. Charlotte Bishop, Flower of the Mammoth Cave."

Later that year, their son Thomas was born. They were very happy.

Free at Last?

As THE 1840s passed, the topic of slavery was more and more in the news. The United States had won a war against Mexico and claimed huge new territories as a result. The Gold Rush attracted thousands of new settlers out west, to California and Nevada. Vast new areas of land were opening up for settlement beyond the Missouri River.

New states were joining the union. Still, no one could agree on whether the new states should be allowed to keep slaves.

At the same time, thousands of immigrants were arriving in the United States from places like Germany and Ireland. These new white Americans took away many of the jobs free blacks had held in the Northern states. It became very hard for many freedmen to support themselves and their families.

The Southern states pointed at the blacks struggling to make a living up North. They claimed the situation would get a thousand times worse if slavery was abolished. Where would all the former slaves find work? Every state, North and South, would end up having to feed, house, and clothe thousands of people, the slave owners warned.

But this argument held no truth for the millions of slaves still held in bondage. Many tried to escape.

Stephen's state, Kentucky, was a slave state. But the northern border of Kentucky is formed by the Ohio River. On the other side of the river were the free states of Ohio, Indiana, and Illinois. Any slave who could cross the Ohio River without being captured could hope to start a new life.

Stephen heard many stories of slaves who escaped to the North. Many received help from the Underground Railroad.

When he first heard the name "Underground Railroad," Stephen wondered what kind of train could run for so many miles below ground. He soon found out that "underground" meant "secret," and that the "railroad" was a network of safe hiding places along the journey from South to North.

All along the way, "conductors" helped the runaways. They let the slaves sleep in their barns or attics during the day and gave them directions for traveling by night.

It is estimated that about fifty thousand slaves reached freedom by following the Underground Railroad. But 4 million men, women, and children remained enslaved. Stephen was one of them.

As time passed, Stephen, Nick, and Mat had made many

amazing discoveries. By now, Mammoth Cave boasted 226 avenues, 47 domes, 23 pits, and 8 waterfalls. The Snowball Room got its name from the beautiful round formations of the mineral called gypsum found all over the ceiling there. Stephen discovered the Rocky Mountains, a huge pile of fallen rock, at the farthest end of the cave. Stephen climbed it to the top, but he could find no passageway beyond.

Stephen had become an educated man. By reading as many books as he could, and by talking to as many people as he could, Stephen learned many things about the world beyond Kentucky. Because Mammoth Cave was so famous, visitors came from France, England, and other faraway countries. Stephen listened to their talk and copied their polite manners. He learned to say "hello," "welcome," and other things in different languages.

People who met him were often surprised that a slave should know so much. Even scientists asked him questions about geology and cave formation. Some of Stephen's customers were writers who published articles about their trip to the cave. Many times they mentioned Stephen. He became the cave's most famous guide.

Many well-known visitors asked for Stephen to guide their tours. The glamorous singer Jenny Lind, who came from Sweden, visited Mammoth Cave during her concert tour of the United States. Stephen led her to a rock formation that resembled a large chair. There she sat and rested for a few minutes. The formation became known as Jenny Lind's Arm-Chair. The violinist

Ole Bull, who came from Norway, gave a concert underground while attending one of Stephen's tours. Stephen also guided Prince Alexis of Russia and Dom Pedro, the emperor of Brazil.

But because Stephen was so famous, he was always in demand. Now he had little time to explore the cave, even though he guessed there were many more tunnels hidden away in the darkness. His tours lasted all day. Visitors could choose between two different trips. The "short" trip took nine hours, while the long one took fourteen!

Stephen made several rescues. Once while he was leading a tour deep inside the cave, a man fainted from exhaustion. Stephen carried him on his back for many miles until they reached the open air. Another time, a man was separated from a tour group and lost for many hours. Stephen found him and brought him back safely. Sometimes visitors staying at the hotel had nightmares about being trapped in the cave. They would wake up screaming for Stephen to save them.

Stephen had a good sense of humor. Slaves did not normally joke with white people, but Stephen knew how to gently poke fun without hurting anyone's feelings. The customers loved to hear him do it!

Years later, his old master Franklin Gorin described Stephen in a letter. Gorin wrote: "Stephen was a self-educated man. He had a fine genius, a great fund of wit and humor. Some little knowledge of Latin and Greek, and much knowledge of geology, but his great talent was a knowledge of man."

That "knowledge of man" served Stephen well. He knew how to calm down a nervous visitor. He knew which men and women could be joked with and which ones would not like it. He knew how to behave in front of royalty and how to talk to scientists. Because he knew more about Mammoth Cave than anyone else did, he was not shy about showing his knowledge. And people from around the world respected him for it.

While Stephen's fame continued to spread, Dr. Croghan was still struggling to find a cure for consumption. The underground hospital hadn't worked, so he tried other experiments. But in 1849 the doctor lost his longtime battle against the disease. He died of consumption himself.

Stephen, Charlotte, and the others were worried. When a slave owner died, his property was divided among different family members. That meant that slave families could be divided as well.

The worst thing that could happen to a Kentucky slave was to be "sold down the river." Plantation owners in the Deep South were anxious to buy more slaves. They needed as many field hands as they could get, to grow cotton, hemp, and other crops. The work was backbreaking, and a slave sent to Alabama, Mississippi, or Louisiana could expect only hard days and a short life.

The city of Lexington was the center of the slave trade in Kentucky. Stephen had heard many sad stories of husbands and wives taken to Lexington and sold to different owners, and children separated from their parents. The newspapers Stephen read were filled with advertisements offering slaves for sale.

When Dr. Croghan's will was made public, it gave instructions for what would happen to the cave, his home in Louisville, the farm called Locust Grove, and all his belongings.

The doctor had never married and he had no children. So he left the cave to his nine nephews and nieces. As for the slaves who lived there, his instructions were that all of them would keep working as usual for the next four years. Then, for the three years after that, all the slaves would be hired out and allowed to keep their wages. At the end of those three years, they were to be set free.

Freedom! Stephen and Charlotte celebrated. In seven years they would both be free, and their son Thomas, too!

But as the days passed, Stephen came to think that seven years was too long to wait. His life did not change much. Almost every day he led a tour through the cave, telling the same stories and answering the same questions that visitors always asked. He still loved the cave, but his work was becoming monotonous.

Some of the people who took Stephen's tours talked with him about slavery. Visitors from Europe told him that slavery no longer existed there. England had freed its slaves in 1838. In 1848, France did the same.

Charlotte collected many newspapers during her cleaning duties. At night, Stephen read from them to the other slaves. They could not be seen gathering together for this purpose, so

At night, he read the papers to the other slaves.

Stephen would visit one cabin or another to read to a small group by firelight. Quietly, they discussed what was happening in their country.

In the United States, people were afraid that the argument over slavery would lead to war. Many Southern landowners warned that they would rather separate from the Union than give up their slaves.

Runaway slaves who reached the North told anyone who would listen what life had been like for them. Frederick Douglass was one escaped slave who became famous. He spoke to audiences all over the North, and his stories of being a slave in Maryland were horrible to hear. His listeners became even more certain that slavery must be wiped out.

Some people thought that the slaves should be sent back to Africa. A group called the American Colonization Society bought some land on the west coast of Africa and began sending freed slaves there. They called the new colony Liberia. In 1847 a former slave from Virginia became the governor there.

The year 1850 was a terrible one for all slaves. That was the year the Fugitive Slave Law was passed in Washington. The Southern slave owners had demanded a new law that allowed them to track runaways even into the free states and drag them back into slavery. Now escaped slaves could not feel safe unless they ran all the way to Canada.

As he prepared for his freedom, Stephen thought about moving to Liberia. He told some of his friends that he might move there and become a lawyer. He was even studying the law. But he wasn't sure. He hadn't been born in Africa—he had been born in Kentucky. Why should he have to move all the way to another continent to live in freedom?

Stephen also heard reports from some of the former slaves who had moved to Liberia. Life there was very hard. The men and women who returned to Africa had to carve a home for themselves out of the jungle. Many missed the lives that they had left behind in the United States.

In the year 1856, Stephen, Charlotte, Thomas, and all the rest of Dr. Croghan's slaves were emancipated. They were free! Stephen had saved every penny that he could. He had even bought a piece of land. Now he decided to buy another one. He would rent the land to farmers who wanted to grow crops there, and make even more money that way.

In 1857, Stephen and Charlotte sold 112 acres of land. We do not know what they were planning to do with the money, because later that year, Stephen died.

No records tell us how it happened. Stephen was only thirty-six years old. Did he become sick? Did he die in an accident? No one today knows for sure what happened. Mammoth Cave holds many secrets, and this is one of them.

The Legacy of
Stephen Bishop

TODAY, STEPHEN BISHOP is remembered as America's first great cave explorer.

Others followed in his footsteps. Cavers from all over the world heard about the finds Stephen made. They came to Kentucky in hopes of making their own discoveries.

As the years passed, cavers brought equipment that Stephen never dreamed of. They didn't have to memorize the twists and turns of the cave, as Stephen did. Instead they used compasses and other tools to measure exactly how far they traveled and in what direction. They wore powerful headlamps attached to helmets and carried all kinds of fancy climbing gear.

Mammoth Cave is by far the longest cave known in the world. Before the 1970s, however, this was not the case, although some explorers suspected it. A few miles to the north, another big cave system, called Flint Ridge, contains many miles of tunnel. If the explorers could somehow find a passage connecting Mammoth to Flint Ridge, it would become the longest known cave system in the world.

In 1972, after many years of exploration, six brave cavers discovered the underground connection. They started from a cave on Flint Ridge. For twelve exhausting hours they pushed through tight holes, crawled under low ceilings, and waded through water. Finally, they emerged in Mammoth Cave.

They found themselves standing in a passageway Stephen Bishop had discovered and drawn on his map. If Stephen had only had more time, he might have made the connection to Flint Ridge himself!

Today, Mammoth Cave has more than 350 miles of explored passageways. Scientists and cavers guess that there may be hundreds more miles of tunnel just waiting to be found.

In 1941, Mammoth Cave was named a national park, and today it receives about 2 million visitors a year. Park rangers guide the tours now, and the trails are lit by electricity. Visitors can see for themselves the stone huts where tuberculosis patients lived, the beautiful Snowball Room—where they can have lunch in an underground cafeteria!—and many other sights that Stephen Bishop showed to visitors in his own time. There are no more boat rides on the Echo River, because the park wants to protect the delicate ecology of the river and its creatures. But a video of the blind cave fish is on display in the visitor center.

If you visit Mammoth Cave, be sure to contact the visitor center in advance and make reservations for the tours you choose, because spaces can fill up early. The website is www.nps.gov/maca/home.htm and the telephone number is 270-758-2180.

One of the most popular tours is the Violet City Lantern Tour, offered during the busy season. The lantern tour does not use electrical light. Instead the guides hand out kerosene lanterns, and the three-hour trip is conducted very much as it was in Stephen's time.

To find out how real cavers explore, take the Introduction to Caving Tour. Visitors stoop, bend, and crawl through passages away from the traditional tour routes. You must be at least ten years old to take this tour. Expect to get muddy and tired!

The Historic Tour takes visitors to many of the places Stephen Bishop showed his visitors: the Wooden Bowl Room, Bottomless Pit, the Little Bat Room, and Mammoth Dome. Steamboat Rock is now called the Giant's Coffin.

There are many other tours to choose from. The cave is open year-round except for Christmas Day.

At the Old Guides' Cemetery near the historic entrance to the cave, you can see Stephen Bishop's grave. His headstone was donated by a Pittsburgh businessman named James Mellon, but it has the wrong date of death on it—1859 instead of 1857. In the visitor center, a brochure describes Stephen

Bishop as the greatest explorer of Mammoth Cave. No other person, in his time or later, discovered more miles of passageways there. Without Stephen Bishop's brave explorer's spirit, Mammoth Cave would not have become the place of wonder it is today.

Stephen Bishop's Life and Times

1821 (?)
Stephen Bishop born in Kentucky.

1838
Brought to Mammoth Cave for guide training
by his owner, Franklin Gorin

FALL 1838
Crosses Bottomless Pit, discovers River Styx

1839
John Croghan, physician from Louisville, Kentucky,
purchases Mammoth Cave and becomes
Stephen Bishop's new owner

1842
Tuberculosis colony built in Mammoth Cave

WINTER 1842
Stephen creates up-to-date map of Mammoth Cave

1843
Marries Charlotte; their son, Thomas Bishop, is born

1849
Dr. Croghan dies. His will directs that all his slaves
be freed seven years later

1856
Stephen, Charlotte, Thomas, and the rest of
Dr. Croghan's slaves emancipated

1857
Stephen Bishop dies under unknown circumstances

APRIL 12, 1861
First shots fired at Fort Sumter, South Carolina, marking the
beginning of the Civil War

1862
President Lincoln issues the Emancipation Proclamation,
which declares that all slaves living in rebel states
shall be freed as of January 1, 1863

APRIL 9, 1865
Civil War ends when General Robert E. Lee surrenders to
General Ulysses S. Grant at Appomattox, Virginia

ELIZABETH MITCHELL was raised in Omaha, Nebraska, but her grandparents lived in Louisville, Kentucky. When she was a young girl, her Louisville grandparents first took her to Mammoth Cave. Many years later, Ms. Mitchell took her son to see the cave. There she noticed the brief mention in a park service brochure of a cave guide named Stephen Bishop. Captivated by the description of Bishop, she began researching his life for a book. She read newspaper articles about Bishop as well as firsthand reports written in the 1840s and 1850s. Modern-day cave guides and the official Mammoth Cave historian also contributed information.

Elizabeth Mitchell is the award-winning editor-in-chief of Del Rey Books, a publisher of science fiction for adults. She and her family live in Brooklyn, New York.

KELYNN ALDER is of Mexican American heritage. She grew up in a peripatetic family that lived in several countries and traveled extensively, learning at an early age to appreciate a wide range of the world's living cultures. Her fascination with people's diverse backgrounds, together with the need to draw and paint, developed into a love of portraiture. Today Alder lives with her husband, son, daughter, and two Bernese Mountain dogs on the North Shore of Long Island.